LOST VOICES OF
CRICKET

GW00455238

LOST VOICES OF
CRICKET

Legends of the game in conversation
with Ralph Dellor
written together with Stephen Lamb

BENE FACTUM PUBLISHING LTD

Lost Voices of Cricket

First published in 2014 by
Bene Factum Publishing Ltd
PO Box 58122
London
SW8 5WZ

Email: inquiries@bene-factum.co.uk
www.bene-factum.co.uk

ISBN: 978-1-909657-50-2
Text © Sportsline Media Limited

Cover and book design: www.mousematdesign.com
Printed and bound in Malta on behalf of Latitude Press

Picture credits

With thanks to Getty Images, The Cricketer International, ESPNcricinfo
Ltd, Hulton-Deutsch Collection/CORBIS, The Manchester Evening News,
Arsenal One Two Five and the ECB.

Every effort was made to locate the appropriate copyright holder of the
pictures in this book. In some cases this has not been possible and no
infringement is intended.

To the memory of the subjects of this book.

It was an immense privilege to meet them and listen to their stories.

Contents

If you would like to hear the voices of the subjects who feature in this book, visit the publisher's website and listen to extracts of the original recordings, free of charge.

Complete original recordings of each individual interview are available for purchase, as will be an audio version of the book.

All details at
www.bene-factum.co.uk

Introduction

THE SEEDS OF THIS BOOK were sown in 1989. It was 60 years since Tom Pearce had made his Essex debut and he had served the club in one guise or another since then. It meant that he had been around for nearly two-thirds of the county's first-class existence. The then secretary of the club, Peter Edwards, a much-respected administrator in his own right, suggested that I might record the thoughts of Tom Pearce on tape for posterity.

He thought that there might be some interest among members to listen to those recollections, so he set up the opportunity for me to make copies of the cassettes available for sale. Interest was greater than anticipated, leading me not only to interview more former Essex players, but also to approach other counties to see if they would like me to interview any of their former greats. The take-up was such that I spent many hours in the company of some delightful characters and great men of cricket, listening to the game's relatively modern history unfolding before my ears, and my microphone.

Each interview had a story of its own. For instance, it was not straightforward arranging to hear Bob Wyatt's remarkable story. He was approaching 90 when I made contact with him, at his home in Helston, where he spent a lengthy period of his final years. I happened to be in Cornwall on holiday and arranged that I should contact him while there, only to find that he was setting off to London for the Oval Test against India. We agreed to meet outside the committee room at tea on the first day, and my intention was to make the recording at close of play. That was not Bob Wyatt's plan. He said that he was prepared to give

1

me the time for the interview, but only at his hotel in London on the Sunday rest day of the Test.

So, much against my inclination for a lie in, early on Sunday morning I made my way to London to meet Mr Wyatt, as his mere presence seemed to demand he was addressed, in his penthouse suite. A hot summer's day would have made his original suggestion of an outdoor recording more attractive, but background noise made that impractical. So we sat inside. It was not long before all my misgivings were overcome by the sheer wonder of talking to a man who brought to life the history of modern, and not so modern cricket. Here was somebody who had conversed—at length—with C.B. Fry and Plum Warner, with Douglas Jardine and Harold Larwood, now conversing with me. Rather than being bothered about driving 50 miles on a Sunday morning, I would willingly have walked 50 miles on Christmas Day, just to listen to this fascinating tale.

Trevor Bailey told me to come to his home in Westcliff, where he suggested we should record the interview and then have a spot of lunch. The 'spot of lunch' lasted well into the afternoon as we chatted about cricket, broadcasting and everything else that came to mind. I make no apology for revealing that Trevor Bailey was my boyhood hero, and to enjoy such an experience was truly memorable for me.

Brian Statham and Cyril Washbrook welcomed me to the president's room in the Old Trafford pavilion, the perfect venue to delve into cricket history. I met Alec Bedser in the Oval pavilion, while Colin Ingleby-Mackenzie welcomed me to his home beside Lord's, as did his dog who made an appearance on the recording. Denis Compton gave his interview actually inside Lord's, which was like his home anyway. I went to Bridgwater to meet Bill Alley in his home. Less grand than the Ingleby-Mackenzie abode, it was nonetheless homely and a delight to be in his company.

Doug Insole I interviewed twice. Once for the original

project, and more recently when I was doing some research into the business of selection. His thoughts on the subject were fascinating and worth, I thought, including in this book, even if they fell outside the strict confines of interviews conducted back in the 1990s.

None of the interviewees were told of the questions in advance, which accounts for the fact that some of their memories were not totally accurate. Where possible, these inaccuracies have been corrected in the written form without losing the flow of the narrative.

Readers can download an audio file from the publisher's website [www.bene-factum.co.uk] that will enable them to hear the voices of the interviewees. This should greatly enhance the experience of reading the book. It is also possible to obtain copies of the original audio interviews.

Thanks are due to Stephen Lamb, who has helped me immeasurably with the preparation of this book. Above all, I must thank the nine subjects who gave willingly of their time, extended a warm welcome to me without fail, and whose voices will live on for posterity.

Ralph Dellor
Newbury, 2014

Bob Wyatt
1901–1995

Bob Wyatt

IT IS ALWAYS INTERESTING to listen to Test captains talking about the game, because they generally have an unsurpassed depth of knowledge. When the captain in question was born in 1901, appropriately at the start of the cricket season, his views demand unparalleled attention.

Robert Elliott Storey Wyatt made his debut for Warwickshire in 1923, playing for the county until the war. In 1946 he resumed his career with Worcestershire, continuing until 1951, although his final first-class match was not until 1957. He captained Warwickshire between 1930 and 1937, and Worcestershire between 1949 and 1951. He led England in 16 of the 40 Tests in which he appeared and in this lengthy career averaged 31.70 in Tests and 40.04 in first-class cricket, with 39,405 runs and 85 centuries. He also took 901 first-class wickets, including 18 in Test matches.

These are impressive statistics, but there is much more to be told about the life and career of one of the outstanding characters of English cricket. Notably, he was Douglas Jardine's vice-captain on the infamous Bodyline tour of 1932–33, and he became England captain in his own right. He was a selector and, as he neared the end of a distinguished life, he became one of the most respected elder statesmen of English cricket. Furthermore, it was not just his longevity that demanded respect. He was not universally popular, for he held trenchant opinions, which nevertheless remained relevant across the ages, and despite the fact that he was in his 90th year when he was interviewed his memory was still razor-sharp.

Born at Milford in Surrey, his introduction to cricket came at a very early age. He could remember walking about with his bat and one pad when aged three. He also remembered being taken to watch his father play for the South Saxons in Hastings by his nanny. They were sitting opposite the pavilion and he asked if he might go to see his father. Rather than walking round the boundary edge, this little chap with his bat and pad walked right across the middle. Looking for all the world as if he had just completed a century, he was clapped and cheered by the spectators. Wyatt Senior looked out to see what all the fuss was about, and saw his young son climbing the pavilion steps. Recalling the occasion, Bob Wyatt commented, "That was, of course, the first ovation I ever received." *He did not need to add that it would not be his last.*

With equal clarity, he recalled the first match in which he played. It was at his preparatory school, Kingswood at Camberley, and he was captain. His side batted first and were bowled out for 11. As captain, he decided to open the bowling himself. He took four wickets in his first over, including a hat-trick, with the result that they bowled out the opposition for 11 to salvage a tie. Not many careers could have started in such a dramatic manner and still spawn stories to top that one.

From Kingswood, he went on to a not very well-known public school, King Henry VIII in Coventry, as a day boy. He was originally down for Marlborough, but his father, "who was a very clever man but a very bad businessman", *lost a lot of his money and could not afford to send him. By that time the family had moved to Warwickshire and lived near Coventry, so he went to a school where the wicket was not too good and the practice wickets were even worse. Consequently, he did not make a lot of progress.* "When I was at prep school I was rather outstanding as a batsman and a bowler for my age, but during the years I was at King Henry VIII during the First World War, I made practically no progress at all. I did finish up by being captain of the XI, but I wouldn't say I was particularly good there."

He joined the Coventry and North Warwickshire club where they had wonderful practice facilities, with the net wickets being every bit as good as, if not better than the wickets in the middle. "The members were frightfully good about encouraging the young, and I used to go to practice nearly every evening. At that time I decided to go in for automobile engineering as an apprentice at the Rover Motor Company, so as soon as I got away from work in the evenings, instead of going home, I went to the ground to practice. I was very much helped by the players there, and by the captain. They had some very good players, three of whom played county cricket including a chap called Freddie Peach who played for Derbyshire a bit, as did Stanley Holden, and also a very good left-arm bowler called Reaney. They were all so helpful and encouraging that I feel I owe that club a tremendous debt of gratitude.

"I used to practice at home quite a bit, because we had a pitch that father and I made. He coached me a lot; he was a very good club cricketer if not up to county standard, and used to tell me how important it was to get in line with the ball. If I didn't get in line, he was displeased. Against fast bowling I was much more frightened of displeasing him than being hit by the ball, and I suppose it was from then that I got the reputation of having guts against fast bowling."

He was pretty successful playing for his club in Coventry, but at that time he did not think he was good enough to play county cricket. He was eventually asked to play for Warwickshire second XI against Derbyshire at Derby, yet hesitated before accepting, telling his father that he did not think he was good enough. "Father insisted that I played and I got about 30 or 40 runs, so I realised that it was not quite as difficult as I imagined it might have been. That's when I think Warwickshire took an interest in me."

Some of the players at his club had thought him good enough to play for the county back in 1921. He did not think so, but there was one member of Coventry and North Warwickshire who was convinced of Wyatt's qualities. He was a member of both Warwickshire and Surrey, who got so exasperated by Warwickshire's lack of interest that he wrote to Surrey alerting them to Wyatt's birth qualifications. In turn, Surrey wrote to Warwickshire asking if they had any intention of playing him and if not, they were going to invite him to play at the Oval.

This was the first time, but not the last, that Wyatt was the subject of qualification disputes. "It rather woke Warwickshire up and I got a telegram asking me to play in the first dozen matches of the following season. I think I was kept out by the fact that old Santall [the coach, Syd Santall] wanted to keep young Santall [Reg] in the side. He didn't want anybody who was likely to dispose of his son. I may be entirely wrong, but I found when I started to play I was good enough for Warwickshire."

So where had the doubts come from? "Modesty! But it is a fact that pre-war, nearly all the good players, all the great players I played with or against were very modest men, from Jack Hobbs down. It's quite different now. I remember a little while before Lord Charles Cobham died, I was sitting talking to him about a certain player who was quite good and Charles turned to me and said, 'You know, if he was half as good as he thought he was, he'd be twice as good as he is.' That has been the attitude of a lot of modern players. They have an over-rated opinion of their ability and I think that if you're going to be a success in cricket you have to have a certain amount of confidence in yourself, naturally, but the ones who are successful are those who are rather better than they think they are."

Wyatt remembered being surprised by that telegram asking him to play in the first 12 matches of the 1923 season. He acknowledged that the Warwickshire committee clearly did not want him to go to Surrey, and the thought that he might forced them to declare their interest, so he appeared for the side for the first time against Worcestershire. He remembered some of his colleagues in the Warwickshire side. "I think I'm right in saying that our opening batsmen were Smith and Bates. Young Santall, who incidentally should have been an England player with the right kind of head on him, Freddie Calthorpe was the captain, he was a good all-rounder, and Billy Quaife, of course, who was a magnificent player and a wonderful example for a young chap to follow. He was the perfect player, correct in every way. He also bowled very slow leg breaks and got quite a number of wickets. By then he was approaching his 50th year but he was still a very valuable player. It was later on that players like Croom and Kilner appeared. I can't remember the Worcestershire side except that Maurice Foster was captain and they had a fellow called Bowley. I'd have to look in Wisden and then I'd remember them all."

As to the match itself: "I think I got 37. I was put in fairly early, but after that Freddie Calthorpe put me on to bowl towards the latter part of the innings and I got a few wickets, so he decided, in my opinion quite wrongly, that you couldn't do both, so I'd be a bowler. The result of that was for the following two seasons

I went in nine and ten. It was a great handicap and halted my progress in batting. I would have got on much quicker in county cricket if I'd been given the opportunity of going in earlier, as I was in my first season. I was not out 13 times and yet I wasn't moved up. I wasn't put in again anywhere else until one season when Freddie Calthorpe was ill and Norman Partridge captained the side. He put me in first against Yorkshire and I made 40-odd, and from that time on I began to develop, with the result that the following season in 1926 I got quite a few runs and I was asked to go to India. In India I got nearly 2,000 runs with five centuries, and then I became a batsman.

"I suppose I could claim to be a genuine all-rounder, although I ought to have been a better bowler. I did open the bowling for England on one or two occasions, which was rather extraordinary. In fact, I think the first time I opened the bowling was in Durban and I bowled 11 overs for one run with one wicket. It surprised me more than anybody else. My wicket was Herbie Taylor, who was one of the best batsmen South Africa have ever had. Then I wasn't put on again until the score was somewhere in the region of 240 and there'd been a partnership of 90-odd runs between Deane and Nupen, and I got them both out in my first over. At one time my analysis was 12 overs, three wickets for one run, which was even more surprising. One of my greatest friends then dropped a sitter off me at mid-off, which would have made my figures four wickets for one run in 13 overs. Eventually I think I finished with 15 overs, four runs and three wickets."

How closely was he following county cricket before he started playing? Were there players who, albeit from afar, he was trying to model himself on, trying to pick up mannerisms from? "I had certain players I was very keen to watch, in particular Jack Hobbs and I am sure I learned quite a bit from him. I was rather interested in watching Hobbs because when I was nine, my father took me to the Oval to see Surrey against Kent, and the main reason for going was that he wanted to see Kenneth Hutchings, who played for England and for Kent. He was particularly interested in him because he had coached him in the Classics and Maths, my father being quite a scholar. He knew him very well, but much to my father's disappointment Surrey won the toss and instead of seeing Kent bat we saw Surrey.

"I can see now Hobbs and Hayward coming down the steps at the Oval, and father told me that man Hobbs opens the batting for England. I thought he was an absolute god and I worshipped him. He was my hero. The interesting thing is that exactly 20 years after that I was his captain in his last Test match. Anyone who had gone up to Hobbs and said, 'You see that little boy; he'll be your captain in your last Test,' it would have been too absurd. I told Hobbs about it and he was very, very amused, because I was captain in 1930.

"I always think of Jack Hobbs as the greatest batsman I ever saw, on all wickets. Obviously he's not the greatest run-scorer because you can't get away from the fact that Don Bradman made more runs than anybody else in a given time. But Bradman never gave his wicket away, while Hobbs did on many occasions, such as when he got 100 and the side was in a good position, he often didn't go for more runs but got himself out. Sometimes he'd see himself at 150 and he'd settle down and go on to get 200, but I'm absolutely certain he could have turned a lot of his 100s into 200s or even 300s and have just as good a record as Don. His record on sticky wickets was outstanding, whereas Don failed on sticky wickets, so I always think Jack Hobbs was the greatest player against all types of bowling on all wickets."

It is often said that true class transcends any era. Was there anything in Jack Hobbs' technique that modern batsmen could apply, or was it just a gift he had that nobody else could emulate? "He had a wonderful ability to judge the length of the ball, which is always important. But one of the things about Jack Hobbs was that he was always in perfect poise, whether he was playing back or forward. Poise is rather more than balance. You can be perfectly balanced but badly poised, but you can't be well poised but badly balanced. I always think that when you are poised you are in such a position that you are able to assume another position rapidly without losing your balance. Even when Hobbs was bowled out, he was in perfect poise.

"The same applied to many. Wally Hammond was another example; all the good players had poise. I used to discuss these things with Charles Fry, who was a great friend of mine, and he always said that poise was one of the most important things, not only in cricket but in all games. Wilfred Rhodes told me a very interesting thing about Jack Hobbs. When I went on my first West Indies tour I would like to spend the evenings talking with Wilfred Rhodes. We had quite an elderly touring party with Rhodes, George Gunn, Andrew Sandham, all approaching 50 and I found them very interesting. I'd much rather spend my evenings talking with them, or rather listening, than going to the pictures, where a lot of the younger members of the party went.

"Wilfred Rhodes told me that he first went to South Africa in the days when they played on the mat, against the famous quartet of Bert Vogler, Aubrey Faulkner, Reggie Swartz and Gordon White, who bowled the googly. Rhodes said that Jack Hobbs couldn't see the googly, while he [Rhodes] could. But he said that when the score was 50, Hobbs would have about 45 of them and he had about five! I asked how he accounted for that and he said the simple reason was that Hobbs knew where the ball was going to bounce much earlier than anybody else. Therefore he was able to get right to it or right away from it.

"I think that also applied to Don Bradman. Eric Hollies bowled Bradman for nought in his last Test at the Oval, as you know. Tom Dollery told me this before the match: 'You know, we don't think Don can pick the googly,' and I replied, 'God Almighty, if he can't see Eric Hollies', he can't see anybody's.' I think that has applied to a lot of the players, and the only real advantage of picking the googly is stroke-making. If you get one a bit short and it's the googly, you hit it on the on-side and if it's the leg-break you hit it on the off-side. In my case I couldn't see them all, but I could see quite a lot. When I was doubtful I just dismissed it from my mind, because it's much better not to think you know and be wrong than to take no notice of it at all. There were times when the sun was behind me that I could see the ball spinning in the air, so I didn't have to look at the hand because I could see which way the ball was spinning. If the sun was the other way and not shining on the ball, I couldn't."

Modern professionals always say that cricket was a different game between the wars in that it was less intense and professional. As someone who played then and watched later, did Wyatt consider it to be so, or just different? "When they say it was a different game, it was better in those days because there was a greater amount of variety. It was played in the true spirit in which the game was intended to be played, it was more chivalrous, and there was no appealing for LBW by square leg. In fact if any of my side appealed for LBW, if they were not the bowler, wicket-keeper or first slip, they got ticked off for it. But now everybody seems to appeal.

"I think players knew more about the game then, about swing and flight. Flight as we knew it in our day has virtually disappeared. Flight is rather more than variation of pace. Bowlers like Jack White would make the ball curl on to you and dip, and Clarrie Grimmett's ball was more like an inswinger because of the spin which took it opposite to the way it turned, and at the same time it dipped. That's why he got so many LBW decisions, because he made the ball dip and then straighten. Instead of being, say, on the off stump, it was on middle and leg. It was the actual spin of the ball in the air which caused it to dip.

"In the same way an off-spinner, if he drops his wrist so the axis is perpendicular, with one side of the ball travelling quicker against the air than the other, it will float away. So a lot of good bowlers in those days bowled their off-spinner and then they'd drop their wrist and instead of the ball coming from the off, it went the other way. People I talk to today don't seem to know anything about it, and it's surprising to me how little people know about what might be termed the mechanics of the game.

"I suppose at my age it's very easy to glory in the past and think everything was so much better than now, but even making allowances for that, I met a lot of old buffers when I played who told me that cricket wasn't what it used to be, and I thought to myself, I would never get like that, but by George, it's difficult not to.

"Fielding has improved. Sides are younger, the throwing is better, and generally fielding is better, although I won't say that there are better fielders than some from the past. I haven't seen a better fielder than Wally Hammond in any position, or a better fielder than Learie Constantine, or Duleepsinhji in the slips, but there are more of them. Why they slide along on their backsides I don't know; I don't think that's an improvement. After all, when they've done that they've got to get up and throw the ball in. I understand all their washing is free, which might make a bit of a difference! There is no doubt that the general standard of fielding is better, but the standard of batting has dropped a lot."

1929 was a marvellous season for Wyatt. His aggregate of 2,630 runs was his best ever, although there were five occasions when he passed 2,000 runs, but it was not easy to get him to talk about a summer when perhaps conditions were particularly favourable, or he was going through one of those purple patches that batsmen sometimes enjoy. "I would say that the wickets were good, but at the same time there were some pretty good bowlers in those days, with the likes of Maurice Tate, Harold Larwood and Bill Voce around. The standard of bowling then was much better than it is today, but there was no question that the wickets were good."

In 1930 he assumed the Warwickshire captaincy. Was that something that just happened or had it been a long-held ambition? Did he enjoy captaincy? "I considered it a great honour and yes, I did enjoy it because it made one think about the game more and I used to think a lot about the tactics and strategy. The awkward part was that I didn't get support from the committee. Nor did Freddie Calthorpe who preceded me. That was a bit of a worry to me, right from the outset.

"I remember when I was asked to captain the side, saying to the secretary that I would be only too pleased to and I would make mistakes, but I would be happy if any member of the committee at any time asked me why I did anything, I should always have a reason for it. I captained the side for seven years and not once was I asked by any member of the committee why I had done anything. There were times when I went up to the committee room and as I walked into the room there was sudden silence. It rather suggested they were pulling me to pieces. It was very depressing."

Wyatt was a successful captain of Warwickshire, taking the county to fourth place in the Championship in 1934, represent-

*ing their highest finish since 1911 when they took the title itself
for the first time. But after briefly reflecting on that, he went
back to his criticism of the committee and the way he was
treated.* "We went up in the Championship, yes, but another
thing that upset me a lot was in 1936 when I had a letter from
the chairman saying that apparently I gave no encouragement to
the young players. I had gone out of my way to help the young
players, and that is proved by the fact that Eric Hollies wrote a
whole chapter in his book about how I helped him in cricket and
taught him cricket. Also, remarks by Tom Dollery, who said I
was a tremendous help to his batting. Again, Aubrey Hill, so
many of them have said so.

"I had charming letters from them when I was kicked out, saying
how upset they were and thanking me for all I had done for
them. I had no claim on the captaincy, because the captain is
elected from year to year, but they could have elected another
captain without accusing me of not helping the young. That was
very depressing and it happened in a letter I received in the midst
of a period when I was out of form—the only time I was really
out of form—and I needed encouragement, not discouragement.
That was a very sad time for me."

*Looking back to happier times, Wyatt was first chosen to play
for England in 1927, following that successful tour of India in
1926–27. India were not a Test-playing country at that time, so
he had to wait for his Test debut.* "We did play an unofficial Test
at Bombay, and we played in Ceylon. I learned a lot on that trip
by batting with Andy Sandham, who was a very fine opening
batsman. He had gone in with Hobbs over the years and was a
beautiful player, again, perfectly poised.

"I was batting with him in Colombo and I hit the ball to deep
extra cover and ran down the wicket calling for a run. When I

got up to the other end, he hadn't moved. I said, 'Come on
Sandy; gracious me that's near on two runs.' He looked at me
and said, 'If you don't get back you'll get run out.' I was a
youngster in those days and got back easily. It happened to be
off the sixth ball of an over and he thought I was trying to pinch
the bowling. He walked down the wicket and said, 'Now look
here, I spent ten years running singles off the last ball of the over
with Jack Hobbs; I'm bloody well not going to do it for you!' He
was a tremendous friend of mine and I was terribly fond of
Sandy, so I took it as he meant it, but I always thought that he
had a tremendous sense of humour.

"That was entirely different to Herbert Sutcliffe, who was on the
South African tour of 1927. We went to play a match at Port
Elizabeth on the mat, and they had a very fast bowler called
Osche who was a giant of a man. He bowled us out for 49 on a
very unpleasant wicket on which the ball flew all over the place.
I remember Ian Peebles coming in and I said to him, 'Now you
get in line and you'll be all right; I'll get down that end as soon
as I can.' Ian got in line and got his bat up by his nose, but the
first ball hit the bat handle between his hands and it went to
gully. He was out and very pleased to go. At the finish it
happened that I was not out 13.

"In the second innings we had to get 187 to win the match. Our
opening batsmen managed to strain themselves, except Herbert
Sutcliffe. Greville Stephens of Middlesex had an imaginary strain
in his thigh or something, and Eddie Dawson of Leicestershire
had twisted his ankle. After my first innings when I was not out,
I was sent in to open with Herbert to face this blasted chap, and
we set about them. I got to 92, I think it was, and Herbert was in
the seventies and he came down the wicket and said, 'There are
only about 14 runs to make, so I won't hit any fours and I'll give
you as much of the bowling as I can, so you will have the chance

to get a hundred.' Now I was a very junior player and he was a very famous player, but I am convinced that a majority of professionals would have much rather been 86 not out and me be 94 not out than me being 100 not out and they in the seventies. I always thought that Herbert was the most unselfish of the great players I ever played with. I am jolly sure that if that had been Sandham, he wouldn't have done that, as nice as a chap he was."

It was on that tour of South Africa that Wyatt finally made his Test debut. As he recalled: "I was LBW nought at Johannesburg. I don't think it was a very good decision actually, as I think it would have missed the leg stump, but the umpire said I was out and when the umpire says so, you're out. But I got 91 in the next match in Cape Town, so I managed to keep my place in the side."

Despite his success on that tour, when he averaged 42.28, Wyatt was unable to establish himself in the side and was always liable to be the victim of selectorial whims. "In 1929 there was the first Test match for many years in Birmingham. By that time I was getting more runs than any other amateur and I thought I stood a very good chance of being selected on my home ground. But I wasn't good enough according to the selection committee, because they played a chap called Tom Killick from Middlesex. He was a very good player, but he failed. I was very disappointed not to have played in Birmingham.

"I may have become rather conceited by then and thought I was good enough, but I may have been entirely wrong. I eventually played in the fourth Test. By that time Killick had been dropped and I got in because Wally Hammond was crocked. I managed to get a hundred in my first Test in this country. Frank Woolley and I beat the third wicket record against South Africa. I always think I was greatly helped then by Woolley, who made things look so easy. He was a beautiful player.

"Then the following year I thought I had a good chance of playing against Australia, but I didn't get in until the last Test when I replaced Percy Chapman. I went in against Grimmett for five balls before tea. I hadn't played against him before, so that was a nerve-wracking business. Not because of me but because of the sympathy of the crowd, I had the biggest reception of anyone on a Test ground to that point, according to Plum Warner who was writing for the *Morning Post*. He wrote, 'Never did Trumper in all his glory in Sydney have as great a reception.' I am not claiming it was due to my ability, but simply because I had been written down by the press. I helped Herbert Sutcliffe to beat the sixth wicket record against Australia, so in my first three Tests in this country I was a partner in two record stands, but then the following year I wasn't asked to play. I think I was a bit unlucky having got these runs in 1930, not being asked to play in 1931."

The selectors showed their fickleness once again in 1933, following the 1932–33 tour of Australia where Wyatt had a batting average of 46.71 in the Tests. When he returned from that tour his place in the first Test went to Maurice Turnbull. But he had been more than just a leading batsman on the Bodyline tour, as he had been Douglas Jardine's vice-captain. Several ideas have been floated as to how leg theory, or Bodyline, came about, but Wyatt was quick to dismiss them and tell exactly what happened. "There's been an awful lot of nonsense talked about that. It was never a preconceived idea, and in fact the first person to set that field was me. I set it in Melbourne when we were playing against an Australian XI and Douglas Jardine went away fishing, leaving me in charge. It was a very, very fast wicket and the ball got old very quickly. In fact that ball is now in the Long Room at Lord's, and it's worth looking at because it's torn to shreds. So the ball ceased to swing away when Harold Larwood was bowling. The Australians, being mainly what you might call right-handed and back-foot players, were playing the ball mainly to the on-side. As the ball was not likely to leave the bat, I moved one slip, then another and then another one to the leg side to stop runs. There was no idea of intimidation or that sort of thing. Harold was bowling very fast and it wasn't very pleasant, I admit. Occasionally he dropped one short, but very, very occasionally. Don Bradman was very worried about it and in fact complained to the Board of Control about our method of attack then. That was a foolish thing to do.

"When Douglas Jardine came back I told him about this, and what I had done with the field and he said, 'That's interesting; we'll pursue the matter.' Those were his exact words."

MCC were bowled out for just 60 in their second innings, leaving the Australians just 125 to win. Wyatt was somewhat perplexed as to why the batting had failed so miserably, until happening upon enlightenment. "I discovered why our batting in the second innings had been so poor. Pataudi had taken the side down to a nightclub. I didn't know anything about it, for I was sleeping peacefully in my bed.

"Anyway, I went up to Harold Larwood and said that we had to bowl these chaps out, because if Mr Jardine comes back and we've been beaten, there'll be hell to pay. He replied, 'That's all right, skipper, I'll bowl them out. He had absolutely ideal conditions with the wind behind him, a slight slope down and it was greasy on top. I've never seen speed like it. I was fielding in the slips next to Bill Voce. Bill said, 'I hope to God they don't snick one; it would go straight through us!' We were only about 30 yards from the boundary and we weren't too deep. Wicket-keeper George Duckworth, who was about ten yards in front, was taking them up above his head, and he said to me, 'Skipper, I'd like to go ten yards further back, but if I do I shan't be able to reach them; they're still rising.' Anyhow, we bowled two out for 19 before it rained and that was that, but we'd frightened Don out of his life. Frightened him out and then bowled him out. Douglas was delighted to hear about this, and that's where the idea of Bodyline started.

"I believe there was a dinner party at a hotel in London, and Douglas went there to talk to Arthur Carr about his bowlers, Larwood and Voce. I think Larwood and Voce might have been there, but it was not with the view to Bodyline. Quite naturally, Douglas wanted to know as much about these bowlers as possible and obviously the person from whom he was most likely to get it would be their captain. That's why they had this dinner party. But the idea of it all being preconceived on the way out on the boat is completely untrue. Furthermore, it wasn't bowled until the second Test match. It wasn't bowled in the first Test when McCabe got a wonderful hundred.

"Larwood bowled very fast and very well then, but not with a concentrated leg-side field. When we got to Melbourne for the second Test, the wicket had been doped so all the pace had been taken out. We had decided to play four fast bowlers and leave Verity out. My argument, quite wrong as it turned out, was that if you couldn't get them out with three you wouldn't get them out with four. We played Bill Bowes, and he did persuade Don to pull the ball down on to his wicket, but it was the only wicket he got. In the second innings the wicket was such an easy pace that the only way of attacking was to bowl bouncers at them, set the field that I had set, and instruct them to bowl at the leg stump.

"That was where it was born really—the second innings of that match, which they won. The Australian press was full of the fact that they'd got the measure of this fast bowling by Larwood and

Voce and everything was going well. When we got to Adelaide on a very good wicket that was fairly fast rather than exceptionally fast, we lost four wickets for 30 runs, so the crowd were buoyed up. I went in at that point having changed places with Douglas Jardine, because he got so worried and was a bundle of nerves waiting to go into bat. The selection committee thought it would be much better for him to go in first. We won the match by 338 runs from 30 for four, and Larwood and Allen bowled magnificently on that wicket. That's when the balloon went up, when Woodfull was hit over the heart by Larwood. Then Douglas very foolishly moved all the fielders to the leg side and attacked with the field he had at Melbourne. It was a foolish thing to do straight away, and Oldfield was hit on the head outside the off stump. It was entirely his own fault, but the crowd took exception to it and didn't like to see their wickets go down."

There was a suggestion in some quarters that Gubby Allen refused to bowl to a leg-side field, but that is another theory that Wyatt dismissed as having no foundation. "Gubby Allen was never asked seriously to bowl leg theory. The rumour is that he refused to bowl to a leg-side field, but I remember Douglas saying to me that Gubby would be very useful bowling his orthodox stuff outside the off stump. And he said, 'When they get down that end having had a dose of Larwood from the other end, they'll try to take liberties,' which they did. That was one of the reasons that Gubby got so many wickets. He bowled magnificently, mind you, and I'm not saying at all that he wasn't worth his place in the side, for he was. One thing that is very disappointing is that Don Bradman, writing his [Allen's] obituary in Wisden, said that Douglas threatened to send Gubby home if he wouldn't bowl Bodyline. That was completely untrue. Can you imagine Douglas Jardine sending someone who was an MCC committee member home, an amateur, in the middle of a tour? It's too absurd, isn't it?"

The Australian crowds hated Jardine with a passion. He had a slightly aloof and superior air, enhanced by a prominent nose that made it difficult, if not impossible, not to appear as if he was looking down it the whole time. There was an occasion when Jardine brushed away a persistent fly with his hand while fielding. From the crowd came the cry of, "Hey, Jardine. Leave our flies alone!" The Australian players did not warm to the England captain, with Don Bradman at the forefront of the movement. How did Wyatt regard his captain? "I was very fond of Douglas Jardine. He was very much maligned. All the professionals in the side were devoted to him. He was always Dr Jekyll and Mr Hyde, but he was a thorough gent in every way. That was my opinion and was not necessarily the opinion of everybody because he was let down when he got back by Plum [Warner]. At the same time, Douglas would not suffer fools gladly, and he couldn't stand insincerity, and I can't help saying that Plum was always a little bit insincere. But I remember having a letter from him [Jardine] when I was captain in 1934. It started: 'Poor Bob, I have the greatest sympathy for you. What with the efforts of Leveson Gower on behalf of Errol Holmes, and the efforts of Plum Warner on behalf of Gubby Allen, the season will prove interesting.'"

It is sometimes difficult when caught up with great events to appreciate the scale of their significance at the time. This is especially true of a cricket tour when it appears that the eyes of the whole world are centred on that tour. Were Wyatt and his colleagues aware of the impact that their activities were having on the wider world of cricket, diplomatic relations and the Commonwealth? "It was brought home to us the influence it was having on the Commonwealth and as far as the cricket [was concerned], I didn't approve of that method of attack. I could see lots of reasons for it with the ball not moving, mechanical

Leading from the front: Wyatt finds the boundary during his innings
of 33 in the triumphant 1934 Ashes Test at Lord's

reasons for it, but I decided it wasn't a good thing because anything that bred ill-feeling in the game must be bad. So I didn't approve, and told Douglas that."

Was this despite the fact that he, *Wyatt*, had initiated the strategy? "I hadn't really initiated the policy, I'd only set the field. I hadn't instructed the bowlers to bowl bouncers at the leg stump. I'd only set the field from the point of view of stopping runs, not to frighten the batsmen. I think if you're a captain you set the field either to get people out or stop runs, and I set that field to stop runs."

Did it not occur to him that the bowlers might take it as being a signal to pepper the batsmen? "I wouldn't say it didn't occur to me, but if there had been a series of bouncers from Harold Larwood I would have stopped it. I think I would have stopped it then. I certainly would have done later on, perhaps when I'd given more thought to it. The whole difficulty really was not so much the bouncer; the difficulty was that they didn't know whether it was going to bounce or not. The wickets out there at that time were of variable bounce."

Back home in domestic cricket, Wyatt had a disagreement with the Warwickshire committee that meant he stopped being captain in 1937. He played for a couple more years up until the war, still with the county. "I played because I thought my loyalty was with the county, and I took the view that it was up to the committee to ask whoever they wished to captain the side. It was only an annual appointment anyhow. What I took exception to more than anything was the accusations made against me, not the fact that they dropped me as the captain.

"Also, I liked all the players. I may say that I was very popular with my side and even today the ones who are left write to me. I had a charming letter from Aubrey Hill some time ago, and from a fellow called Wilmot and they're delighted to hear from me. I was going to play after the war for them, but we had a president whom I can't say I ever liked. Dr Thwaite gave a luncheon party in the hotel just before the season started in 1946 and I was invited to it, naturally. One of the committee members left early. As he went out of the room he said, 'Good afternoon gentlemen, and Mr Wyatt.' I thought, 'If that's the attitude, what's the point of playing for them anymore?'

"Worcestershire were very keen for me to play for them. I had a qualification in that I'd lived in Worcestershire for two years at the beginning of the war, but I made the mistake of not notifying Warwickshire of my intention to play for Worcester. So it was void, really. I said that I could go and play for Surrey, and Errol Holmes was most anxious that I should play for them, and in fact captain Surrey after the war. I didn't particularly want to go, because it meant upheaval as far as my home [was concerned], and also I couldn't afford to play regularly, rather about half the matches, mainly home matches.

"So I thought I'd play for Worcester. When I told the Warwickshire committee about various things I didn't approve of, and how I thought it would be better for everybody if I left and went to play for Worcestershire, they had to sign an approval form for me. They refused to sign it. The first thing I did was speak to the MCC secretary, Raitt-Kerr, and he said I could get in by this registration which was brought in to get county cricket going. All I had to do was get my county to sign that they did not require my services any more. I went back with the form, but they wouldn't sign it. I said that if they didn't, I would put out the story as to why I was leaving Warwickshire. They signed it straight away."

Once the release papers were signed, Wyatt joined Worcestershire for what he referred to as a happy final phase of his career. "It was a lovely ground to play on and terribly nice people. Mind you, I'm not saying the Warwickshire committee aren't nice as they've been frightfully kind and hospitable to me since the war, but it is composed of different people, and the secretary Leslie Deakins was a tremendous loss to Warwickshire and a very great friend of mine.

"Worcester at that time were charming. I always remember I played some four or five matches, and I usually arrived about the time they were going out to field, as I was fairly busy in those days. One day I arrived in plenty of time, and I was sitting in front of the pavilion with Maurice Jewell, who was then chairman. He had played for Worcestershire, and he said to me, 'When are you going to get a hundred for us?' I jokingly said, 'Well it's a lovely day, what about today?' He said that if I did, he'd give me a tankard. I got 150 not out. Then I went back the following week and played against Gloucestershire and I got 154 not out. He said to me that would do for the time being because he couldn't afford to get any more tankards inscribed. I said it was a pity, because I thought I might get another that day. I got one soon after, 177 off Alec Bedser, the first time I'd seen him. I keep on reminding him about it. But I've still got the tankard inscribed with the two scores."

Wyatt finished playing for Worcestershire after the 1951 season, but he continued to play the odd first-class match through until June 1957, when he made his final appearance for the Free Foresters against Oxford University in the Parks at the age of 56. He scored only 1 and 6 as Oxford won by 187 runs, but he had the very respectable bowling figures of 10-4-28-0. Two years earlier in another first-class match he appeared for D.R. Jardine's XI against Oxford University at the Saffrons in Eastbourne, taking his 899th first-class wicket in the process. He remembered the details: "It was M.J.K. Smith. He thought he could hit an away swinger over mid-on, just where I wanted him to hit, and it ended up in cover's hands."

Even after he finished playing he remained in close contact with the game, becoming an England selector and chairing the committee for a time. Did he enjoy that? "I enjoyed it up to a point but to be perfectly honest, I would have liked more intelligent people on the committee than I had. There were certain people who didn't know enough about the game to be selectors, in my opinion. Later on there were more, like when Len Hutton came on, and Leslie Ames, he was a good selector. I thought that some of my fellow selectors lacked knowledge of the game, and knowledge of the mechanics of the game.

"I would have liked to have been on with Gubby Allen, who was more of a theorist then than he used to be. Gubby only became a theorist after his 1936 tour to Australia. He used to rather scoff at theory, but a lot of new players were getting out to very moderate leg-break bowlers. I wasn't playing at the time because I had broken my arm, but I said to Gubby, 'It's perfectly obvious what's happening. In this country the wickets are harder and the ball has a steeper bounce. They were getting caught at mid-off, caught and bowled and caught at cover.' I said that you have to get nearer to the pitch; it was as simple as that. Gubby looked at me and said, 'Oh, you're all bloody theory.' I said that may be so, but if your theory is correct, it can always be put into practice. He asked if I thought my theories were always correct, and I said that I'd be a bloody fool to have a theory that I didn't think was correct.

"By the time he was chairman of the selectors he was a great theorist, and also enjoying it because it's terribly interesting. I used to talk theory with Charles Fry a tremendous amount in Australia, when I had this broken arm and I wasn't able to play. He was the greatest scholar/athlete of all time. He knew so much and wrote that book on batsmanship which is one of the best ever on the subject. That's something lacking today, I think, the theoretical side of it. And it's quite true: any theory that is correct can be put into practice."

Wyatt said that Jardine would not suffer fools gladly, while giving the impression that he himself would not suffer them at all. "I don't hit back. Douglas would let a chap know; I would keep it to myself."

But he was not surrounded with fools but a wide panoply from all walks of life. "When I think of the people I've met and not only in the game, but followers of the game from the Royal Family down. Hundreds of delightful people. It's an education too, or used to be an education on how to behave, but I'm a little bit doubtful now. And of course, it's a very healthy life, healthy exercise, but in my day the professionals didn't make any money out of it and the amateurs made less. I never made any money out of it, but I have had experiences I couldn't get in any other way. I have very many happy memories, of course."

Wyatt suffered a mild stroke in 1994, but still managed to get to the Lord's Test against New Zealand that year. He died in 1995, just two weeks short of his 94th birthday. In obituaries and eulogies, it is often said that we will not see the likes of him again. In the case of Bob Wyatt, that sentiment is most certainly true.

Bill Alley
1919–2004

Bill Alley

*B*Y THE TIME MOST *cricketers reach the age of 38, they have enjoyed the best part of their careers, and are just playing out time, or have even retired. It was at the age of 38 that William Edward Alley began the serious part of his first-class career, if the word 'serious' is the right one to express the enjoyment Bill Alley brought to the game.*

He had played first-class cricket before—12 matches for his native New South Wales between 1945 and '48—but he had also done a number of other things. For instance, he was a professional boxer, winning all 28 of his welterweight contests. He had played Lancashire League cricket with Colne from 1948 to '53, and spent another four years with Blackpool before entering county cricket with Somerset.

Never a man to leave a job half done, he proved to be a sensation. In 1961 he scored 3,000 runs at an average of over 56, as well as taking 62 wickets at just over 25 each. In all first-class cricket, he scored 19,612 runs at 31.88, and took 768 wickets at 22.68. He retired in 1968, just six months short of his 50th birthday, and went on to the umpires list, where he remained until 1984.

Going back to the beginning, where did his cricket start? "A ground back in Australia, a little place called Hawkesbury River, a little oyster and fishing village, and I got in with the local team. I used to run around the field, and I was so small I wouldn't bat.

They wouldn't put me in to bat on this concrete, matting wicket, but eventually I started to develop, and I had some sort of swashbuckling technique, and I enjoyed it, and went on and went on, and then I went up through the grades."

Did he come from a cricketing family? "No, my father didn't know a cricket ball from a tennis racket. I had four brothers, but they never played, two sisters, but anything at all with a ball, I sort of co-ordinated. I had a ball sense. Even now, I suppose I can hit a golf ball as far as anybody, with a wood, but if you tell me to chip a ball 25, 30 yards, I hit it 60 yards, no chance in the world of putting it anywhere near the hole! I played a fair amount of first-class tennis out there, and I played rugby league, but when it came to the round ball, soccer, I used to kick it with my toe. I couldn't understand these fellas kicking it on the side of the foot, and of course that went out. But when I came to England, and I ended up playing at Blackpool for four years, I came across this great player, Stanley Matthews, and I used to sit there and watch a lot of these matches, and I used to think, when one man can kick a ball and put it from one foot to the other, right from one side of the field to the other, it was magnificent, it was an art. You see, Stanley couldn't play cricket, and I used to argue the point with Stanley about it, but any ball game seemed to come to me, click, just like that."

What about the boxing? Was there ever any danger that he was not going to play full-time cricket, and that he was going to be a full-time professional boxer? "Well, I suppose at that stage in my career, we had a chap out in Australia, he was a lightweight champion of Australia, Dick Patrick. I went to school with him, and when he was boxing he said, 'Why don't you come down to the gym and have a bit of a spar?' I was working on the railway at the time, working in a tunnel, on a big jackhammer. Silly, stupid, big fella, big arms, and they put me on this position on this railway job! But anyhow I went down, and I started to train, and they said, 'Oh, you'd better go and have this fight, have that fight.' Of course, in your first few fights you didn't know the fellow you fought, but he came from the same gym! I remember in one particular fight, I went into the ring and looked at this fella, he had a broken nose and I thought I'd never seen him before! But I realised after the referee said, 'I want a good fight because you both come from the same stable,' and of course I didn't know this, and I knocked this fella out in the second round, and never seen him after! But I went from this to that, and had a go at anything!"

But cricket came to the fore, and in 1945 he made the New South Wales state side. "Yes, it was a different kettle of fish then, because it had become more serious. Playing in the New South Wales team at the time, they were winning everything. The first time I played for New South Wales was in Brisbane, and it was 30 bob a day. Miller and Lindwall and these fellas, they earned hundreds, but I enjoyed it. I was never coached. We had an Australian New South Wales coach, and he used to say, 'Let him play his own cricket, just let him go on, and he can hit the ball,' and I scored a terrible lot of runs, but of course at that stage, when the Test teams were picked, around about that date, the Bradmans and the Browns and the Hassetts and the Barneses, the O'Reillys and the Lindwalls and the Millers, you had to be an exceptional cricketer to play Test match cricket.

"It wasn't until the '48 tour, Bradman's last tour over here. I made such an impression just before the tour was picked, that I had this contract to come to play league cricket with Colne in Lancashire. I didn't know what to do, and Bill O'Reilly said, 'You get across there, you'll be a sensation, the way you play. What are you, 28? If you stop back here, how are you going to play? What are you going to get out of it?' He and Stan McCabe had a big sports business in Sydney, and McCabe said to me, 'Look, you'll be in the next team to be picked. I can't guarantee it, but I'm almost assured that you will be.' The contract was worth only about £700, so Bill O'Reilly said, 'Never mind about that, you get across to England,' so I took his advice, and honestly I've never looked back. I came across, and I got more money for 22 weeks of the year, when they played one day a week!

There was the thought that he should have been in the '46 team that went to New Zealand. "That was another thing; only Bradman had more runs than me at the time on the circuit, before that team was picked. I was looking forward, because when I was down in South Australia, Bradman said to me, 'All you've got to do is keep yourself in first-class condition, and you're on the trip.' Well anyhow, when we came back on the Saturday morning, there were headlines on the back of the Telegraph, big three-inch letters, 'Alley Tragedy!' People were ringing up, they thought something had happened to me, I'd committed suicide or something like that, but it meant, 'Alley Tragedy—Left out of the Team.' And of course they took this fellow Ronnie Hamence, who was a brilliant player in Australia, but a failure under those conditions.

"I was excluded, but up till then I was so assured, I went to a firm and I got a dozen pairs of cream flannels, beautiful cream flannels, cream shirts, all ready for the tour, thinking I was going to be on it after what Bradman said. And then of course, when I've seen this in the paper, I thought, 'Oh God, blimey, I've got all this stuff here.' Anyhow, there was a bloke playing for the same club as me, Ernie Toshack, and I went in to see McCabe about this business of it being in the paper on the Saturday morning, and when I came back, the wife said, 'I've given all that stuff, the cream pants and the cream shirts to Ernie Toshack.' I said, 'What for?' She said, 'You said he could have them, that you wouldn't be making the tour.' I'd never said a word to him about it! But I was very disappointed about that, because it was the big tour coming up. I was lucky around that time, I was invited to go on a lot of tours, and I was the only New South Wales player, the rest were all Test players, even poor old Clarrie Grimmett and these fellas were going. But they used to take me for the experience. I suppose it's the biggest disappointment of my career, that I've done everything else in the game, and been very lucky through it, but not getting the green cap."

After the snub, he came to England to play league cricket. Was there a chance of playing county cricket when he first came over in 1948? "I'd no intentions whatsoever, because the thought was that I wanted a three-year contract, which they gave me. I thought if I'm a failure in the Lancashire League they gave you a kick in the backside and away you went, but I was very lucky to jump into the stride and I scored, I think, 1,000 runs, which in 22 matches was very good, and I kept on getting a contract. I only left Colne for the reason that we were getting all the Australians and West Indians over in the league at the time, and we were playing Sunday cricket. Colne had a couple of old stodgers concerned with the league that were against sport on Sundays, they said, 'Look, we're going to stop our professional, Alley, from playing on Sundays, he's going away to other clubs.' I was going away into the central Lancashire league and we were making a terrible lot of money. We had our own team, own chara, own blazers and caps. We used to play the West Indies in every other match, and it was like Test matches! The Weekeses, the Worrells and the Walcotts were playing, and the Ramadhins and the Valentines—you can tell what sort of matches we were playing. And then I said, 'Well, if you're going to stop me playing and earning money, you start playing Sunday cricket.' But of course, they wouldn't hear of it.

"Blackpool got to know about this, which was the biggest cricket club then in the Northern League, and so under darkness they got me down to Blackpool, and a fella by the name of Grime, who was a millionaire and ran the local paper, and anyhow we talked business actually, and a chap who used to run the waxworks at Madame Tussaud's in Blackpool, he was my spokesman. I put my price, and he said, 'Oh, you're worth more than that, mate, you want to give this fella another £400!' Well £400 then was a lot of money, and we were well over the thousand pounds, Everton Weekes and me.

"So I went to Blackpool, where I had a three-year contract, and then they gave me a one-year contract, and I was winning the league and the cup, and loved it, and I wanted a longer-term contract. Lancashire wanted me to go there early on, Ken Grieves, another Australian was there at the time, and then Leicester offered me £500. I said, 'Look, I've got more than £500 in collections!' But £500 to go to a county was still a fair price then, so I said to Blackpool, 'Now look, I'm married with two young children. I want some security, a three-year contract.' No, these old codgers said, we can't give you three. Of course, age was starting to come into it then, and they thought, 'This fellow's going to break down! He plays every week. Everything's been all right since he came to England, but the time's going to come with his age, he's going to break down and cost us money.'

"So then Ben Brocklehurst, who used to be captain of Somerset, a big gentleman farmer, got on to me the year before the break in my contract with Blackpool, and I wouldn't do it. Then there was Warwickshire, then there was Kent, then there was Northampton, Nottinghamshire, they all wanted to know if I'd come and play county cricket. I got a bit frightened about this. I thought, my age must come into this now, going into county cricket's going to be six or seven days a week. I've had a pretty run at the mill, so I said to Blackpool that I could go to a county, that was in the last year of my contract then. I went up to Newcastle, to play against a team up there, and of course Harold Stephenson, the Somerset player and captain, was playing and said, 'What about coming down to Somerset?' I said, 'Well I don't know, Blackpool has looked after me pretty well, and I'm getting good money.' So he said, 'Well, keep it in your mind.' Then Brocklehurst got on the 'phone for three quarters of an hour, used to drive me mad. Anyhow I went to Blackpool in my last year and said, 'Look, I want a longer-term contract, or I'm going to take up a professional job with Somerset or another county.' They begged me to accept one year and said, 'You'll be here for ten years!' I said, 'That's no good to me, I want security.' But anyhow they came out after the meeting, and said, 'Sorry, we'll give you one year, Bill.' So I immediately rang Somerset and came down within a fortnight, and looked over a house, and never regretted it."

If Blackpool had given him that three-year contract, he might not have been in county cricket at all. "Well, I couldn't see that far ahead. If I'd been in my twenties or something like that, most likely I would have jumped at it. Harry Makepeace was the coach at Old Trafford, and he said, 'I'd like you to come down and have a talk about playing with Lancashire.' So I went down and he said, 'If you come here, you're too aggressive. I like my players to play on the back foot. You're on the front foot, and you want to attack every ball.' I said, 'Well, it's this way. I've travelled 13,000 miles, I run a good car, own my own house, I've got two kids and a wife. I've done pretty well, and people seem to enjoy the way I play.' Anyway, Harry showed me this very, very good contract, there was no doubt about it, and Roy Tattersall said, 'What are you going to do?' I said, 'What do you think? I've got to calm my game, play on the back foot?' So I tore the contract up in front of poor Harry, and he pulled the chain on the toilet, so I said, 'Well, that's the finish of Lancashire County Cricket Club.' I found the name 'Somerset' more appealing, and when I came down and met the officials and some of the players, I thought I'll give it a try, because I had a three-year contract. I never regretted it for one minute."

"It was just after the Wellard, Gimblett eras. Brian Langford, Harold Stephenson was captain; Graham Atkinson, Roy Virgin came just after, and we had a lot of characters. They were the swashbuckling team of the country. They played because they loved the game, and winning didn't come into it."

Somerset were always noted for having a lot of characters in the team and it was no surprise that he fitted in rather well with that sort of set-up. "Well I did, actually, because the moment I focused there, I was the overseas player in a way, and they said, 'We don't want too much of this.' I said then, 'These clubs want someone to brighten them up a little bit.' I used to walk down from my home in town, and people would say, 'What is it, a two-day game today, Bill?' They never expected us to win, and we developed a team, we were scoring 400 by half past four, quarter to five, but we couldn't bowl a team out. Brian Langford was taking 100 wickets a year, but he'd come as a batsman. If he'd put more time into his batting when he was with Somerset, I think he'd have represented more, because he only played in two MCC matches."

The fact that Somerset were not bowling sides out must have put a lot of work on him. "I had to be in a game of cricket, this was why I'd made myself an all-rounder. Coming to England, in league cricket, I bowled a lot more, because you had to open the bowling, even if you were a leg-spinner; you opened the bowling with the new ball. If you took six for 30, you got a collection of £50, which was a lot of money. If you got 50 runs, another £50.

I'm not being big-headed, I never touched my wages while I was in league cricket, I just lived on collections. Petrol was very, very short the first time I came to Colne, and a mill owner said to me, 'I'll give you all the petrol they'll want for that roller.' I used to sit on that for hours, and if we were playing against West Indies pros, I used to make a real green wicket, plenty of water, plenty of rolling, and of course the ball used to come straight through. If we were playing against a good fast bowler, anything like that, I'd shave it all down, as rough as hell, no grass, take all the shine off the ball, it was pro against pro, it was dog eat dog, no doubt about it. But I developed this medium-pace bowling. They used to say, 'How mean are you as a bowler?' And I used to say, 'Well, I'd never give my grandmother a full toss on her birthday!'

"When I came into county cricket, it helped me this much, and I used to love to bowl to Tom Graveney, Peter May, and Colin Cowdrey. If I bowled them a maiden over I used to think I'd saved 15 runs, and even in latter years, I got more enjoyment bowling to these class players than I got in scoring 50. When Tom was in the nineties, before he got to 100 centuries, I used to bowl to him, and he'd push it back, mid-off, mid-on, mid-off, mid-on, and I'd say, 'Hit me over my head, Tom, you're a class player! I'm only bowling straight!' And he said, 'Well, you might be bowling straight your bloody end, but it's doing something up mine!'

"I think he was on about 96 or 97 centuries, at Gloucester, and his brother, Ken, was there. Our club president used to say, 'Anybody who gets Tom Graveney out, two pounds!' I put two mid-ons for Tom, because he used to hit through there a lot, across the ball but straight. I had him caught out there many a time, including this one, and as I came through the gate afterwards, Ken said to me, 'You crafty old—!' I daren't say it here—and I said, 'That's cricket, that's cricket!' I loved the bowling part of it, and used to field in the gully, and took an enormous lot of catches for Somerset there. I used to be a great talker in the gully; I talked the batsmen out, which people say is unsportsmanlike. I used to get wickets at the other end, because they tried to knock me out of the way at the gully!

"One Derbyshire player, a schoolteacher actually, a very dry sort of fellow—Charles Lee his name was—came in to bat at Buxton one day. He took guard—Fred Rumsey was the bowler—walked straight over to me in the gully, and said, 'I don't want to hear one word from you until I've finished my innings.' So I thought, 'Great, he's taken it to heart!' I had to wait until he'd got 28, and he got out, and he walked past me and said, 'You can bloody talk now, Alley!'"

Some players obviously did object to the talking, but did they generally take it in a good-hearted way? "I've been sent to Coventry by many a team for talking. When I've been at the wicket, I've talked to the 'keeper behind me, and Keith Andrew said, 'I don't know how you ever play cricket.' I remember at Northampton in 1961, the year that Kenny Palmer and I had done the double, and we both got hundreds in this particular match. Keith was their captain, and said to the players, 'Now don't talk to this fellow Alley, just bypass him. If he stops in long enough, walk around him,' and they had two paths either side, where they were walking around me when I was batting. When I got the hundred, Keith said to the lot of them, 'Well, talk to him now, we'll try to get him out now by talking to him!'

"Yorkshire, when Phil Sharpe came in, I used to talk to him. We were playing at Sheffield, and they were all up on the balcony, Closey and all of them, and Phil's talking out of the side of his mouth. I said, 'Who are you talking to, Phil?' And he said, 'I'm talking to you, but I don't want to talk out of the other side of my mouth, because Closey'll see me, and he won't have me in the team next week!' A lot of them used to do this, but afterwards we used to have a joke and a beer, and everything like that. It was a different kettle of fish than what it is today, we enjoyed it then."

Mention of matches against Yorkshire leads to the assumption that he might have had the odd little set-to with Fred Trueman, as another of the game's great characters. "I ended up stopping with Fred after starting to play county cricket, and we used to bring him home here for meals. I used to open, and Fred opened the bowling, and he was a real raw devil then. In a match at Headingley, I pulled up at the ground, and I used to bring the bags. I had a little Morris Minor, and I used to put all 14 bags in—they used to call it the sackswagon actually—anyway, I came to the gates, wound the window down, and a little kid came up and said, 'Are you Bill Alley? Our Fred's going to knock your bloody head off today!' Of course it was one of the Truemans. Anyhow we went in, and Fred bounced his first ball, and it wasn't very good, and I just pulled it for four, up the hill near the scoreboard. He's standing right up, three yards from me at the time, he's rolling the sleeve up another notch, and he used to wear his pants up over his ankles, he was a real red raw-boned fella, no doubt about it. Mind you, he was quick—you didn't know where they were coming from. Then he bowled me a full toss, and I just leaned on it, and of course they run away all the time at Headingley. And he said, 'You kangaroo so-and-so,' and I said, 'Where are you going to bowl the next one, if you do, I'll hit you out of the ground!'

"Then Willie Watson came over, and said to Paddy Corrall, the umpire, 'Have you ever heard a fella batting and talking the way he is, this Alley? I've never heard anything like it in my cricket career!' And Paddy said, 'I don't know if I'm umpiring! I'm listening to him and I don't know what's going on!' Anyway, from that particular match, Fred and I became the closest of friends, and we've had some great fun."

Alley's great year was 1961, when he scored 3,019 runs and took 62 wickets as well. Did he start off like a train, or did it gradually develop? "The first three innings, I started off with two ducks and a one, I think it was. I was pepped up. I was approached by a doctor, actually, to take a certain tablet, as a guinea pig. Anyway I took this pill over the season, and the more the season went on, the more runs I was getting, and the more energy I seemed to have. I can honestly say, away from home, I was very seldom in bed before one or two o'clock, and sometimes later. I was either batting or bowling the next morning, and never felt tired, in any way whatsoever. I built up such a reputation within myself that I couldn't fail. I said once

Bill Alley in action during his record-breaking year of 1961

or twice that I wouldn't have cared if Wes Hall or Charlie Griffith had been on each other's shoulders, they wouldn't have got me out.

"In a particular match at Nuneaton, I scored over 200 on the third day, on an atrocious wicket—the groundsman would be sacked now if he prepared the same sort of wicket. Jack Bannister was a bowler, and Mike Smith and these fellas, and everything they bowled at me, I just whacked through the covers, or pulled, when other batsmen were all failing around me. We lost the game, but out of the 389 we had to get, I got 221. If I'd been headstrong, I think I would have become, with Jim Parks, the only player to score 3,000 runs and take 100 wickets. But the captain, Harold Stephenson, used to say to me after I'd got a lot of runs, 'Well, you're not bowling, you've done your share.' Irrespective of how the game is, we never had a team to win a Championship, so it didn't make any difference. It was only when we lost the toss and were in the field, that I used to bowl. Otherwise, with the 60-odd wickets, I would have got a hundred, no doubt about it.

"But they talk about the '61 year. I backed myself in '62 to be the oldest man to do the double, which I did easily. I think I was somewhere round about 125 wickets, and over the thousand runs, and they don't say anything about that. I took 30-odd catches in the gully, and I think myself that that was a far better year than '61. It was one of these things that I never got up the next morning and said, 'By God, I'm tired.' We played benefit matches on the Sunday, and I never missed a match, I used to love it."

Did he ever discover what was in those pills? "No. They were supposed to be put on the market, and the last match I played I knocked the tablets off, and I never felt one thing different. But the point was that I had so many people ring up, from 17 years of age to 80 or 90, some of them, because they were troubled with arthritis, and lumbago, and all the aches and pains you get in your body, they thought these tablets would do them good, but they never did. But I see the same doctor now, just on and off."

In his benefit year, 1961, he had played against the Australian tourists. What sort of reception did he get from them? "Not very good, because they never come lightly. If you take the record of nearly all the Australians, McCool and these fellas when they played over here, we all got runs against them, because naturally you put your mind a little bit harder to what you're doing. They had a fella, Gaunt, playing on that tour, and he had a terrible tour up to the Somerset match, he even asked Richie Benaud to send him home. I got 135, I think, and a 90-odd, but the point was, this fella Gaunt bowled me one, and I played at it, and of course it went through, and they all appealed like they do. I stood my ground. I knew, definitely, that I never hit the ball, it went through my side. Poor old Johnny Arnold, who was a bit deaf, gave me the credit and said not out. Well of course, over they went past me, all the slips and everybody, and I was the biggest so-and-so that lived, and all this, and of course we never spoke, the whole three days.

"Then I go down to Hastings, and I wanted something like 206 in two matches against the Australians and someone else, to get this 3,000, and I got another hundred against them down there. And then I went on, and I got this 3,000. Then I went back to Australia afterwards with the wife, and I went into this club in a place called Woy Woy, where Alan Davidson came from. Before I came into first-class cricket, I used to live in a place called Hawkesbury River; they're only 20 miles apart. I went into this big club, and there were 800 poker machines in it, upstairs, downstairs, and one bloke just seemed to come out of the blue, and he said, 'The man that's never out's here!' And of course wherever I went, they used to say it, and I knew the papers had given me hell. Even when they come back now, they've still got tongue in cheek."

Alley never made the Australian team to go on tour, but he played for Commonwealth XIs and went on a number of private tours. "I went on about seven or eight tours actually, with Freddie Brown and Ron Roberts, Alf Gover; we were the first to take a Commonwealth team, the Australian team, out of this country to India, Pakistan and Ceylon. Mind you, they were hard. In the first Commonwealth tour, I think we had about eight Australians in the team at the time, two or three Englishmen, and a couple of West Indians, including the great Frank Worrell. Just before we left, we thought it would be a good idea to have a meeting in Bury, and then play someone at Lord's. Freddie Brown was taking a team to Australia at the time, and we wrote and said, 'Look, we'll play you at Lord's before you go, we'll give 50% of everything to charity, and we'll take expenses.' And Freddie Brown said, 'Not on your bloody life, we don't want to leave this country with one win against us.'

"That tour, we played nearly every day. George Duckworth was the manager, and when we were supposed to have a day off, he used to put a game in and reap the benefit, but we loved it, we never complained, nobody broke down. I got a double century on a concrete wicket in Bombay. A game on a turf wicket was washed out, and they took us over to this school and we played on a concrete pitch. It played up with my knees terrible; of course I was getting up again in the old age group. When I came off, I had a knee like a balloon, so they called in the doctor, a bone cracker I called him, and he felt around, and I think he said cartilage trouble. So I said, 'What can you do, Doc?' He said, 'Well, you're not playing tomorrow, so I'll come and pick you up. Come to my house and we'll have something to eat, and then I'll look at your knee.' So I said OK, and he comes and picks me up in a big Mercedes, takes me to this magnificent house, palm trees all over the place. Lunch arrived, and we all sat down on a big carpet, and there was all this milky made-up stuff that to me had gone bad. You roll it up in your fingers, and ate it, and I was nearly sick doing this, and I had to tell him I couldn't eat this sort of thing.

"We went into his surgery, and he must have had someone in there before me, because there were a couple of blood swabs around in a bucket. So I was sitting in a normal chair, and he said, 'Drop your pants down to your ankle,' so I pushed them down, and he went over to a glass chest and came back with a big lump of cotton wool and a bottle, most likely it was ether. He rubs it all over my knee, underneath my leg, and we're talking about the tour and one thing and another, and after about ten to 15 minutes he came over with a little silver needle, and poked it in my knee, and said, can you feel anything? I said, 'No,' so he said, 'It's all right.' So he went back to this glass case again, and came back with a scalpel in his hand. So I said, 'What are you going to do?' 'Ooh,' he said, 'I'll have that cartilage out in two minutes, you'll be right as rain in about three weeks.' I said, 'You what?' And he was just about to stick this knife into me. And I said, 'You are bloody not, Doc!' I never pulled a pair of pants up so quickly in all my life!

"When I came back to England, it was a hell of a mess, so then I had that taken out, and went on and played through it, and then I eventually had the other cartilage taken out, and a couple of ligaments taken out, and then I started umpiring, and then I had a lot of trouble in the knees themselves. So I had them X-rayed and everything, and the specialist said, 'Well, I think they'll have to come off. You'll be all right without them, but they're all honeycomb, they're all gone.' So I went and had this first one taken out, and his houseman was an Indian, and of course he knew me playing out in India and Pakistan when I was out on that tour. I said to him, 'When I come out of the operation, Denis Compton had his knee in pickle; I'd like to have the kneecap in pickle.' After the operation, he said, 'No, I couldn't find a big enough piece; it was all rotten underneath, terrible.' And then I had the other one taken off, and then of course I started to umpire, and I started to get a lot of pain, and I went to see the specialist again, who said, 'If you allow them to go any further, you'll be in a wheelchair. I advise you to have new knee joints put in.' So I said, 'What's it like?' Well he showed me, and I thought, 'Cor blimey, he's never going to put that in my knee.' Anyhow I had both of them put in seven years ago, and never ailed a thing from that day to this."

He continued playing for Somerset until1968, by which time he was very nearly 50. It must have been incredibly hard to keep playing county cricket full time at that stage. "I was tightening up. Mind you, it used to take me a couple of overs before I could really get to the wicket properly. I enjoyed it. I used to be first on the ground of a morning, although I wouldn't go and practise much, I didn't believe in it. If I did go out, I used to bowl two overs at my normal pace. I tried to do what I was doing in the middle. If I went and batted, I used to hate batting in the nets for practice, and Brian Langford always used to bowl off-spinners at me, and I used to lap him and lap him and lap him, but it was the same shot I would play in the game, I never altered. A lot of people play net practice different to what they do in the middle, which I think is completely wrong.

"I used to love it at the finish, I made a few bob because the big papers used to ring me up each year and say, 'How old are you?' I said, 'A year older than I was last year.' And they'd make up a story about my age again, and send me a little cheque. Even when I did the book in '68 when I finished, *Incredible Innings*, Reg Hayter said to me, 'I've been rung up. They want to know your right age.' I said, 'Well, they'll pay for it. It's going to cost you £500 to know my right age.' If I tell them the truth, they still won't believe me. Cec Pepper, who never played county cricket and became an umpire, a real character, he used to say, 'Bloody hell, Bill, what age certificate does that come from? You're on your third, that was in the second one.' I remember the great Scobie Breasley, the rider, he went for years and years and they thought he was a lot older. Not very long ago I was talking about this age business, and I said, 'Well there's one fella that's going to cremate me when I leave this earth, an undertaker, and he's going to do it free, provided I give him my right age before I die, so he can put it on the box.' But it's in Wisden actually, 1919. Even in Australia, they still don't believe it. I remember playing in Sydney, when Richie Benaud used to be brought to the ground in a pram, to watch his father bowl, he used to bowl leg breaks. When we see each other at Test matches, we have a giggle about this. He's another bloke that doesn't age. He's a fair age, Richie, but he doesn't show it."

What finally made him give up playing county cricket for Somerset? "Sunday cricket was starting the following year, and they wanted me to just play one-day cricket. By that I would have lost a terrible lot of money. I couldn't have continued, just playing Sunday cricket, and they thought it would be more beneficial just playing one-day cricket. I called three or four meetings with all the top brass at Somerset, and I never had a meeting with them. From that day to this, we've never come to any conclusion. I only had a fortnight between that and going on the first-class umpires list. I had one or two offers from three counties then, and I thought to myself, 'Well, they'd have to give me three years, and I think I'll give this umpiring business a go,' never thinking that I'd become a Test match umpire. I thought I'd just go on and have a few years umpiring, and enjoy that.

"I had to knock the whole lot out of my mind the first match I had, 'I'm an umpire, not a cricketer.' It was Middlesex v. Essex at Lord's. Peter Parfitt and John Murray, John Price, they all done me, they dropped their sweaters after the fourth or fifth ball, they knocked the pebbles out of my hand, at one stage I didn't know if I was giving eight, nine, ten balls, and I put my hand out and nearly caught Freddie Titmus at square leg. When I came off, Billy Griffith, who was the secretary, said, 'Why didn't you catch him?' They had the knockers on me, and that lunchtime the other umpire, John Langridge, a gentleman, great player, came over to me and said, 'You'll be all right when you get lunchtime over.' I said, 'John, you can wring my jumper out, and my shirt, I'm wringing wet!' I was sitting at the table, I said, 'I can't eat that, I'll have to go into the umpires' room.' Anyhow, he came in and talked me round. I was ready to get rid of it, straightaway, because everything seemed to be out, counts and everything. Parfitt was a devil, actually. When they'd bowled five balls on one or two occasions, they'd walk up, meaning to say it's over. And I'd think to myself, 'Is that five, or is it six?' In a match at Warwickshire, David Brown, the captain, said to me, 'How many have we had in this over, Bill?' I said, 'Why, how many have I got up to?' He said, 'Nine, so far!' And two wickets had fallen! I said, 'Ah well, that's over,' and they accepted it. They wouldn't accept that today. I can honestly say I don't think, in the last ten years of my career, umpire and cricketer, that anybody's enjoyed themselves more than I have over that period."

How much did it mean to him to make the Test umpires list?
"Well, when they rang me up and told me I was on the first-class panel, I thought to myself, 'Well, that's another feather in my cap, this is great.' When they rang me and said, 'You're on the

Test match panel,' and that was against Australia, I thought to myself, 'I've achieved something that a lot of people have never achieved.' I remember Billy Griffith, when we were coming down the steps at Lord's, saying to me, 'Bill, is there anything in the game you haven't achieved?' I said, 'Well, I never played for Australia, there were a lot of good players around at the time. I'd like one thing to happen before I finish this game now, and that's to umpire a Test match here at Lord's, against Australia, with the other Australian umpire, Cec Pepper.' He said, 'God, Bill, never! We can never have the two of you.' He was that sort of man, Billy Griffith, lovely fella. Of course Cec got on the first-class panel, and after he'd been on three or four years, he thought he was better than Dickie Bird and one or two others, and should have been on the Test panel. They never put him on, and of course he chucked the job in."

If it was hard umpiring in that first county match at Lord's, what was his first Test match like? "Well, I was unlucky enough, I suppose, to have Ian Chappell, he was the captain. And they had Thommo and Lillee, and they gave me real hell. If I no-balled Thommo, in particular, a very sedate sort of player, he never said much to me, but Lillee gave me the hard time that I was an Australian. They did give me hell, but I can honestly say that when I walked off at lunchtime, both Thommo and Lillee walked up and put their arm round my shoulder, and said, 'Well, you've weathered the storm.' And then I went on and umpired for a couple of years, and then I was put off the panel, and then I was brought back again for the next Australian tour, and told I was on because I was a strong umpire. At Leeds, where Boycott scored his hundredth century against them, I gave him not out. That was diabolical; the Aussies didn't want to know me at all. I came back and said, 'Look, I've come to England, I think I've made a name for myself, I've made a bob or two, I'm well off, and I'm going to stop here.' I used to say, 'You Aussie buggers,

Alley, in 1972, during his umpiring days

you can get back to Australia as soon as you possibly can.' But if I went back there now and walked on the Sydney Cricket Ground, they'd still snub me."

That must have saddened him. "Yes, in a way, because the New South Wales Association, when I came across to play league cricket, that year, there was so much young talent they had in Australia, behind the big boys, to follow on, that we left, to come and play league cricket. After being here five years, I think it was, I went back, went to the cricket ground, and of course I didn't have any money, and I said, 'I don't suppose you know me, but I've been in England for four or five years, and I played for New South Wales, and Petersham, and I've just come back with the wife's family, and we thought we'd come and watch a bit of cricket.' And the chap said, 'I'm very sorry. You go through that turnstile and if it clicks, I've got to put the money in.' I'm standing there, and of course Miller had come from Victoria then, and he was playing with New South Wales, and he's seen me through the window. I said, 'There you are, that's Keith Miller, he wants me to come through.' And this fella said, 'I'm sorry, I can't let you through,' and he's done the right thing. Anyway, Miller came down and he had a handful of tickets, got me through.

"It was a funny thing, on that particular day, a bloke who used to be captain of Randwick Cricket Club, he's seen me, and he said, 'Come into the bar and have a drink.' I said, 'Oh, I've got the wife with me, and the wife's mother.' 'Today is the first day women are allowed in the Long Room!' So I walked in, had a couple of beers, the eclipse of the sun was on, and Boycott was playing on Sydney Cricket Ground number two. Now, mentioning Boycott, when I was going to finish with Somerset, he said to me, 'How would you like to come and play for Yorkshire?' This is the only time I've said this openly. And I said,

'It could never happen, an Australian playing for Yorkshire.' He said, 'I'll be captain of Yorkshire shortly, and if they don't go with other counties and get an overseas player of some description, Yorkshire won't be Yorkshire cricket, for a long, long time.' Now I always wish that I'd said to Boycott, 'You put that in writing,' because it's past, you've got to believe what I'm telling you, I've never spoken about it after."

He might have been shunned by some Australians, but he always had a very warm welcome in Somerset, and everybody was delighted to see that he was still around at the County Ground, watching Somerset, and enjoying his cricket. "Yes, it's a very good thing because for five years I kept away. It was very hard. I got a funny feeling when I used to pass in the car, I wouldn't look sideways at the ground. I didn't have anything going this way, 'There's a cricket match in there, why don't you go in?' It happens with old players of different clubs, a lot still don't go to their clubs. But now I like to go down there. I don't want to be made a fuss of, I go and sit in the corner of the Stragglers, and have a pint and a sandwich, and I want to be left like that. I go through the gate with my car now, and the old chap salutes me, 'Sir Bill's arrived!' but I've enjoyed every minute of it, lovely."

He spent his declining years in a neat little bungalow in Bridgwater with his wife, enjoying retirement together. There was little that he could add to a lifetime during which he had been a cricketer, umpire, boxer, railwayman, builder, blacksmith, and dancehall bouncer; that is what they call a colourful career.

Trevor Bailey
1923–2011

Trevor Bailey

"COME ON, EAT YOUR *greens or you'll never be able to bowl like Trevor Bailey." I can remember my father saying that to me when I was a young boy one Sunday lunchtime, and the fact that he could think of no greater incentive to induce me to tuck into the boiled cabbage shows in what high esteem Trevor Bailey was held by at least two generations of Essex followers. But either there was still a nasty green mess left at the side of my plate, or there is rather more than dietary considerations to becoming a first-rate bowler.*

Of course, there was more to Trevor Bailey than just his bowling. He was by his own definition a true all-rounder, able to command his place in the side by virtue of either batting or bowling ability alone. Trevor could make this claim at both county and Test level, all the while being an outstanding close fielder and possessing one of the shrewdest cricketing brains in the game.

Born at Westcliff in 1923, he made his Essex debut in 1946 and was awarded Blues at Cambridge in 1947 and 1948, and by 1949 he had gained a place in the England team. He played in 61 Tests, scoring over 2,000 runs at an average of very nearly 30, and took 132 wickets at just under 30 apiece. His performances for Essex were phenomenal. Eight times he completed the double of 100 wickets and 1,000 runs in the season. Once, in 1959, he scored 2,000 runs and took 100 wickets to become the only player to achieve that since the war. To judge his stature in cricketing terms, just consider what would be said of a man who, in the modern game, could score 28,641 runs at an average of 33.42, and take 2,082 wickets costing no more than 23.13 each. Add 428 catches and you have the picture of the complete all-rounder. He captained the county from 1961 to 1966, and from 1954 to 1967, when he stopped playing, he was secretary as well.

By any measure that was a remarkable career, but what stood out as the achievement that gave him the most satisfaction? "I think probably the highlight was regaining the Ashes in 1953, because the Australians had held them for about 19 years, and even Australians felt that we might have a chance. It was a superb series and strangely enough we didn't win until the last Test match, with the other four all drawn, mainly through the weather but I think we had the better of two matches and they had the better of two. I think probably they were the better side."

If that series was a highlight in a distinguished and eventful career, where did his cricket begin? "I started playing on the beach, or shall we say the mud, at Westcliff, where I've lived all my life. I was very lucky that I went to a prep school [Alleyn Court] which had a young headmaster taking over from his father, who had just died. Denys Wilcox had just come down from Cambridge, was also captain or joint captain of Essex, and at that stage in his life was to go on to become a very good headmaster, in fact an outstanding headmaster, but at that time he was very much orientated towards sport and he coached me quite superbly. I followed Essex and watched them a lot before the war. Chalkwell Park was just round the corner and the school very sensibly would take us to watch cricket. I loved that and I've been watching first-class cricket since 1932, when I was very small."

His father played a bit of cricket but was keener on tennis, while his brother could have played most sports but, according to

Bailey, was fairly lazy and did not play very much seriously. So when did it first dawn on him that playing about with a ball was a lot of fun? "From about the age of three, I suppose, or possibly earlier than that, but certainly by the time I was five I was spending my life hitting a ball or kicking a ball. People used to say, 'which game did I prefer, cricket or football?' My answer was always the same: 'Cricket in the summer or football in the winter,' and that is how my life went."

There does not appear to have been any danger that he was going to do anything else apart from being a sportsman, but that is not necessarily how it appeared to the young Bailey at the time. "Immediately after the war, my idea when I went up to Cambridge was to get a degree and then become a schoolteacher. Then Essex offered me the chance to become assistant secretary, I got a tour and from then on my life went round to cricket—but I was going to be a schoolmaster."

Before Cambridge he was at Dulwich College, which was a good cricketing school, and that gave him the background he needed to go on and become a first-class cricketer. "I arrived at the school at the age of 13; I was 14 in my first summer term and we had a pretty good side. We started to win matches and then came unstuck against an MCC side. They had a young Middlesex player called Jack Robertson, who scored 100, and they decided they needed another quick bowler and plonked on me. I had no idea that I was going to play in the first team, having been playing in the colts, and I went into the side and played for the rest of the season as a fast bowler, simply because there was no one else. That summer I made my first appearance for Essex Club and Ground, captained then by Brian Caster who was the secretary, and I couldn't believe his language! I also played for the Essex Young Amateurs, so cricket became my life."

Having watched so much cricket from a young age, were there any heroes or players on whom he modelled himself? "Morris Nichols and Harold Larwood, while from a batting angle I rather liked the look of a little man called Don Bradman, whom I was to see quite a lot of later in life. Anyone who finished his Test career with a batting average of 99 was pure genius. He was a marvellous player. I only played against The Don on three occasions, and on each he got a hundred. I was only glad that I bowled against him when he was well past his peak, because he must have been murder to bowl at when he was really going. He was a magnificent player."

So did he model his bowling on Larwood and his batting on Bradman, or was it just a case of admiring from the boundary? "Admiring them from the boundary, and nothing else. I used to fiddle around with my action quite a lot. My bowling was fairly natural and as for the batting, I was very lucky to be extremely well coached at Dulwich. We had a master in charge of cricket, 'Father' Marriott, who played for England; we had Billy Griffith on the staff. Graham Parker had played rugby for England and played cricket for Gloucestershire and Cambridge University, and we had at least four masters who were minor county players plus two professionals, so it wasn't a bad basis. The greatest thing of the lot was that Father Marriott used to bowl his leg breaks slowly in the nets and then flat in the middle, so one learned how to play leg-break bowling. I've always enjoyed batting against leg-break bowling rather than anything else, and he was a great bowler. He was good enough to play for England as a leg-break bowler, so it was marvellous practice. In the nets he bowled it slow like you get in school cricket, so it taught one to use one's feet and then when he played against the school, as he did for the MCC and the masters and so forth, he bowled it flat and you played him from the crease. We had beautiful pitches, not just in the middle but in the nets as well. I've always believed it's better to have good pitches in the nets than in the middle. I was very fortunate in that, when I went up to Cambridge, Fenner's was absolutely beautiful and although I got some runs up there, it was learning to bowl against really good batsmen on perfect wickets which helped a great deal."

Before going up to Cambridge, Bailey joined the Marines during the war. He said he had a "good war" simply because he made it through while so many of his friends and colleagues did not. It was, however, not at all good when he drove past a recently liberated Belsen concentration camp, an experience that left a lasting impression on him. He could not explain how he came through unscathed, apart from acknowledging that, "The Marines were a very strange outfit. They decided I would never make a sergeant, so they thought an aesthetic second lieutenant would be a better job. I reported down in Wales near Towyn, in a place called Llanegryn. The officer in charge said, 'You are now in charge of landing craft'. I'd never even seen a landing craft, and then having spent about a year and a half training people into landing craft, they switched me to infantry, so it was an odd war."

An odd war, but he did get the chance to play some cricket? "We came back from Germany when the war was over, and I got invitations to play in a lot of matches. I went to my commanding officer and said, 'Could I play in this game and that game,' and he looked at a quite imposing list and he said, 'What you really want to do is disappear for six weeks. We can't give you leave money, but you can disappear,' so I disappeared, so it was marvellous luck for me that I could just depart for that length of time.'

"I played for the British Empire XI, the Navy, Combined Services, a whole host of teams. That was my first encounter with Keith Miller, who at the time was in the RAAF, and I always remember he arrived down in Sussex, and I think I was playing probably for the Navy. I got some runs and Keith came on to bowl. I knew he could bat, but I didn't know he could bowl, and nor did the wicket-keeper. He ambled up off about five paces with the wicket-keeper standing up. It was down the leg side and I don't know who was more surprised, me or the wicket-keeper, but it went for four byes. He was the fastest fifth change bowler I've ever encountered in my life. I was very lucky on one occasion to bat with Wally Hammond. He scored a hundred while I scored 13, but I could watch the master at work and he was a superb batsman."

Such exposure to top-flight cricket obviously stood Bailey in pretty good stead when he went up to Cambridge after the war. "I'd played for Essex in 1946, but not all the time, because I was teaching. I got an early release from the services to go and teach, which I was very pleased about, because otherwise I would have been hanging around for a very long time. I taught for a year and during the holidays I played for Essex, so I'd already played first-class cricket when I went up to Cambridge, and it was simply a continuation.

"We were much older than the university sides are now. Nearly all of us had seen service, and I don't think we had one person who had come straight from school, so we were 20, 21, 22 or 23, even 28, so we were much more mature as people as well as cricketers; we'd been through a war. It wasn't a great side but we used to get draws against the counties, we got hundreds against them and we occasionally beat them; it was not a walkover for the counties."

Doug Insole was at Cambridge at the same time as Bailey, and throughout their careers they became closely associated with one another, playing for the university together, for many years at Essex and even with England. But their first meeting was not on the cricket field. "I was going to play football, and I saw a man kicking a ball about in one of those khaki sweaters, and I thought he was a young pro, but it was Doug Insole. He became the inside right and I played outside right, so we formed the right wing for Cambridge.

"He said he played cricket, and I bowled at him in the nets. I think he was the worst net player I ever encountered, but we all make our mistakes in life. I said, 'He's never going to make any runs,' and he went away. He wasn't in the side, but played for the Crusaders and never stopped scoring runs, so they dragged him back into the side and he never stopped making them. He kept on hitting straight balls through mid-wicket, and I couldn't quite understand why until later, but he was a marvellous competitor and had a good eye. He was a good player."

The universities could compete with the counties in those days and the students took their opportunities seriously, but it did not stop them from having fun at the same time. "I think one of the great moments was when we had a man called P.B. Datta, who was a little slow left-arm bowler from India. He was very slim and fairly light-skinned with black curly hair. When we were playing Somerset, our twelfth man came out with some drinks roaring with laughter, and he said he'd now heard everything. Two old gentlemen were watching when we were in the field and said, 'You know, these Indians are very, very lithe. They open up right-arm fast and then go on bowling slow left-arm.' We did look alike, but it was an extraordinary business to think that you can open up right and then bowl slow left-arm. That would be the complete all-rounder."

As mentioned, Bailey had already made his Essex debut by the time he went up to Cambridge, but could he remember any details about his first match for the county? "It was against

Derbyshire at Ilford, and I opened the batting and I opened the bowling. I opened the batting with a man called Leonard Clark. It was a fine experience. Bowling was Bill Copson, who was at the end of his career but he had the same sort of action as Les Jackson who came on later. Then there was 'Dusty' Rhodes, who became a leg-break bowler, but at that time was still opening the bowling as a seamer."

It appears a little strange that a young man making his debut should have opened the batting and the bowling. "I think we were short of opening batsmen, and that is something which went on all the time. I liked opening, and it never worried me. The only time I didn't like it was if we had been fielding all day and then had to open, especially if you'd been bowling, but it's a strange thing that I was pressed into opening the batting for England more than I was for Essex. Peter Richardson, who opened a lot for England, has got innumerable pints of beer over the years by asking, 'Who did I open with most of all for England?' People say Pullar and so forth, but in fact it was me. I don't know how many times we opened together, but I would say at least ten times and probably more."

In fact the answer was 15 times, but was he successful as an opener? "Not really. I wasn't a good enough player. I should never really have opened, but we were simply short of openers. Ironically, we talk about making mistakes in selection today, but we've always made mistakes. The side we took on my first tour to Australia had seven pure batsmen and of those seven only one was not an opening bat, and that was Denis Compton."

Mention of the fact that Essex were short of opening batsmen in 1946 leads on to the observation that the county was a bit short of most things at that time, not least money. "We have generally been short until recent times, and the introduction of the one-day game on a big scale. It started with the Gillette Cup, but we were struggling for money. The first Gillette Cup game we played was up in Lancashire, and we met the Lancashire secretary Geoffrey Howard outside the police station at Altrincham at 12.30 at night, because that's when we got there. It was marvellous preparation for a one-day game starting at 11 o'clock the following morning! We were put up by him and the players, as we couldn't afford hotels. I think I paid the players £2 a night to put up one of our players. It was a fine arrangement, but how things change."

Things did change, especially for Essex, but it took time until the county became one of the more affluent and successful teams in the Championship, as well as in the one-day game with its associated income. Before that, and before they had their own county headquarters in Chelmsford, perhaps they were regarded by some as the poor relations of the game. "I think there were a lot of counties who were struggling financially, but we had a tremendous amount of fun because we played everything in festival weeks. We had no nets, and once your pre-season nets were over that was our lot, apart from if we were playing at Worcester, Lord's or another county with those facilities. We got our practice in the middle, and that's what you had to do. If you didn't get runs in the middle, you didn't get runs.

"Unlike a lot of players, I always enjoyed nets very much indeed, and I was always trying to have a net whenever possible, but with Essex you just couldn't. We were playing six days a week, normally there was a benefit game on the Sunday, and although the benefit game wasn't hard work, they still started before lunch, went on all day and you had to get into whites. But it was the travelling by car all over the country, sometimes five to six hours after a match if we were going any distance.

"The story I loved concerned Brian Caster, who was a former Essex secretary. He was a lovely man, autocratic, but I adored him and to my mind he was very humorous, even if he could be a bit blunt at times. Essex played first of all at Clacton so Doug Insole and I sent him a card: 'Dear Brian, having a lovely time at the seaside at Clacton'. Our next game was at Scarborough and we sent another card saying: 'Having a marvellous time by the seaside at Scarborough'. We then had to travel from Scarborough to Weston-super-Mare for our next game, and we sent him a card saying: 'Great by the sea at Weston-super-Mare'. After that game we had to drive back to Southend and that was his fourth card, but it shows there was a lot of travelling."

At the outset of Bailey's career with Essex the captain was Tom Pearce. He was a stalwart of the county as a player, captain, chairman and then president. He is perhaps best remembered by the cricketing public for running T.N. Pearce's XI at the Scarborough Festival, but in every respect he was quite a character. "Yes, Burley Tom was a delightful captain who used to stand in the slips. He was a good, gutsy batsman, a forward player who played very straight, and nothing ever ruffled him. His great instruction if we were chasing runs was, 'Go in there, play your shots but don't get out.' It was a lovely, nebulous instruction which I loved. He was great fun to play with.

"I remember Dickie Dodds, who was a lively opening batsman against the quickest bowling, and who used to hit the ball along the ground on the up, and if it was short he hooked instinctively, but he was not a great fielder. On one occasion, Essex put down rather more chances than even we normally did, and Tom had a few words to say to Dickie. He addressed him fairly sharply, which was very unlike Tom, and Dickie replied, 'Sometimes, skipper, you provoke me to wrath.' That finished us and for the next ten minutes we couldn't stop laughing, and that included Tom.

"We enjoyed our cricket, and particularly in the '40s I think this applied very much to the crowds who came to see us. The crowds could be pretty big, but they came to watch cricket after a rather ugly war. The players wanted to play cricket, and we did have a very good time. They liked us to win, but if we lost they came essentially to watch cricket rather than to watch Essex or Middlesex or whoever. And they came to watch players. They came to watch Compton, and they wanted to see him score runs; we didn't, so it was a combination of the personality, the side and cricket.

"Playing festival cricket, the crowds were different. One or two faithfuls went everywhere, but there was still petrol rationing going on, so they couldn't get to all of them. Trains were difficult and our matches at Clacton we used to call an away game because we had to stay down there, and then we called our matches against Middlesex or Surrey home matches, because those were the two matches we would go to by train."

At the start of his cricketing career, Bailey was a promising footballer. "I loved football, but I was brought up in a rugby school. I played a lot of rugby, and then when I went into the Marines it was a bit of a waste of time below divisional level. But you could play soccer at platoon level and enjoy it, so I went back to soccer which I think was always my first love. I played for Southend United reserves quite a lot because it was close by, and I got a lot of experience there. Having come down from Cambridge I went to the manager, Harry Warren, and I said, 'I'd like to play for your reserves. I'm down from Cambridge and teaching, but I can have Saturday afternoons off, but there's one thing—I must have a game every Saturday.' He said that he was awfully sorry but that was impossible, because he had 32 full-time professionals on his books. They were in the Third Division South at the time, so I went to play for Leytonstone and after that for Walthamstow Avenue, and thoroughly enjoyed it. We never played before small crowds, and I can't ever remember playing at Leytonstone or Walthamstow on Saturday with less than 7,000 people, and for the FA Cup and Amateur Cup considerably higher, with 100,000 people at the Amateur Cup final.

"I think the most remarkable one of the lot was with Walthamstow Avenue, when we had a very good run in the FA Cup. We knocked out a couple of professional sides, one from the Third Division North and one from the Third Division South, and we went up to Manchester United, who at the time were probably in the middle of the First Division. Very fortunately we got a draw up there, and they realised that they couldn't possibly get the crowd into the Walthamstow Avenue ground, which held a maximum of about 12,000. So we went to Highbury, midweek, 2.15 kick-off, no floodlights, with a crowd of 55,000; different world.

"Though I loved football, I spent five years playing rugby and so I didn't develop the little things, like a double shuffle and little technicalities which I think I might have acquired between the ages of 14 and 18, which are formulating years, and my heading was never as it should be. But I missed that, and so I knew I was never going to hit the highest spots with football. I think if I'd played nothing but football I'm quite sure I would have played rather better, but I enjoyed it enormously, perhaps even more than cricket, because it was only 90 minutes, and a Saturday, as far as I was concerned, was a tremendous day.

"The best football matches of the lot were always on Christmas morning. That was absolute perfection, because you played and then went back to Christmas lunch. Walthamstow Avenue used to play Leytonstone in front of a big crowd. It was a great occasion and I loved it. I eventually decided to give football up after I had two overseas tours on the trot, and I'd obviously put on some weight and realised I'd been lucky not to damage myself playing football seriously, and I gave it away. I thought, 'What am I going to do on a Saturday afternoon?' but I didn't miss it at all. When I stopped playing cricket I knew that I wouldn't miss it. I was sorry obviously, but I knew I wouldn't miss it, because I knew that if I didn't miss football I certainly wasn't going to miss cricket."

Bailey said that he gave up football when he was selected to go on England tours during the winter, but when did he first get an inkling that he might be good enough to play for England? "I think I decided I was going to be good enough when I was about 13, or even a little earlier than that as far as I was concerned; it was merely a question of time. I suppose the first time I realised I was in with a chance was in 1948, because the Australians simply murdered us and we did need a quick bowler. There weren't many around, as in county cricket the bowling was pretty weak apart from the spinners. There was going to be a chance.

"Then I was asked if I would like to go to the West Indies if selected. I was at Cambridge and I said no, which was the right decision because it would have meant another year at Cambridge. The following year there was a trip to South Africa, and again I said no, so I realised I was being thought about. It came as a surprise obviously when I was eventually chosen, and I never really expected it to last as long as a decade."

Bailey had a good chance to see the 1948 Australians at first hand. "I first played against them at Fenner's, where they murdered us. I got a slight pull and didn't bowl very much, and shouldn't have played, but at the back of my mind was, 'If I get five wickets here I could be in the Test side, or at least I've got a very good chance of getting there.' Showing my complete naivety, I then travelled with them down to play against Essex at

Southend in their coach, as there were transport problems. That was the great 721 all out in a day, which was a fabulous performance. I'd never seen anything like it, nor had anybody else, and we should never see it again. They never slogged, but simply went along making a quiet 200 a session.

"Keith Miller didn't get many that day. I think what really occurred was he got a lot against Leicester, and he was in with a chance of getting 1,000 runs in May. It was the Whitsun bank holiday fixture, and he was always very keen on his batting, more than his bowling. He didn't bat against us at Fenner's if my memory serves me right, and I think he resented being put in as low as he was at Southend. He came in and I simply bowled a straight ball, the stump came out of the ground, much to my delight. I turned to the Don, who was batting at the other end, and remarked that Miller didn't seem very interested. All he said, typically Don, was, 'He'll learn, he'll learn,' and I was just grateful he hadn't learned already, because that was one of the few pleasant moments in that particular contest.

"I learned a lot from the Australians in 1948, because until that time I thought I was going to be a fast bowler. Having seen Lindwall and Miller bowl, I realised I was never going to get anywhere near that pace. So that winter I cut one whirl out of my action, and got myself what I considered to be a disciplined run-up, and completely reorganised my action. I knew I was too wild with the old action, which was all right at times, but I hadn't got the control. People talked about bowling at the wicket, but I always reckoned after that that I was going to bowl at a specific stump. I wouldn't have got the control necessary to do that with my old action."

On that day at Southchurch Park, Southend in 1948, Bailey remarked that Miller did not seem interested in hanging around to score runs. Perhaps he was making a point to his captain or, if other theories are to be believed, he wanted to get back to the pavilion to learn the fate of a horse he had invested in, or even that he had an interest totally outside sport back in the team hotel, to which he wanted to return without further delay. Whatever it was that caused Miller not to linger, Bailey had a more honourable reason for lifting his bat to be bowled by Ray Lindwall in Sydney in 1955. "We'd won the series, and it was marvellous to win in Australia, and I don't know, I had about 70 or 80, and Godfrey Evans said it would be nice if Lindwall got his hundredth wicket, because at that time it looked as if it could have been the end of his career. It wasn't, and somewhat ironically my own career was to be ended on the next tour with a pair, courtesy of Ray Lindwall at Melbourne. He was a great bowler, the best swing fast bowler I'd ever encountered. A great cricketer."

Bailey remembered that match, but he had a reputation for forgetting the details of individual matches. That being the case, how well did he remember his Test debut against New Zealand in 1949? "I remember my first Test in that I got some wickets [6 for 118 from 32.3 overs in the first innings], which was a good start, and it was at Headingley. The thing I remember most was the following day, which was the Sunday. My wife had come up with me, and we were staying in the middle of Leeds, and I got a bad attack of hay fever, which I used to suffer from, sneezing all over the place. We went for a little walk and Leeds is not the greatest place to walk, we hadn't got a car and I saw a bus going to Harrogate. I said, 'Ah, the seaside!' We jumped on the bus and my wife looked at me rather surprised, and when we got off at Harrogate I couldn't see anyone with buckets and spades. I suddenly realised that Harrogate isn't anywhere near the coast, but then geography was never my strong subject."

The Test sides that he was playing in seem to be littered with the names of the great stars of the generation. Was he aware of that at the time? "No. I don't think you ever are. The trouble is that you look back, and you say I played with Hutton, Compton, Barrington, Trueman and Statham, Laker, Titmus, Lock, Loader, Graveney and Dexter, and it sounds absolutely marvellous. In fact is not quite as great as that, because some of the players were at the end of their careers and some were at the start. You always remember them at their peak, and not when they were going downhill. That's why you look at some of the sides and they look terrific, but it can be very misleading. You have to look at a specific year and see what was actually happening. I think the 1954 side in the West Indies was generally pretty good, but there were weaknesses."

That team had the likes of Hutton, May, Compton, Graveney, Evans, Lock, Laker, Statham, Trueman and Bailey himself. Willie Watson was also a member of that side, as he had been in 1953 during the celebrated Ashes campaign. It was at Lord's during that series that Bailey and Watson shared an epic fifth wicket stand that salvaged a dramatic draw when all had seemed lost for England. Chasing an unlikely 343 to win, England slipped to 12 for 3. Watson and Compton stayed until the close of the fourth day, but prospects appeared bleak for England when Compton fell on the fifth morning with the score on 73. That was when Bailey joined Watson in a rearguard action that added 163 runs, but more importantly occupied some four hours. It was only broken when Watson was out for 109, after five and three-quarter hours at the crease, while Bailey soon followed after a four-and-a-quarter-hour vigil that produced 71 runs, but enabled England to survive.

Bailey remembered the background to his determination to stave off defeat. "It was probably irritation more than anything else. Watson was batting with Compton and I hadn't even gone in, and I thought it was a bit hard to be written off that we'd lost

Bailey reaches fifty with a four off Johnstone during the third day of the final Test against Australia at the Oval, 1953

the Test match at that time. It was an interesting operation that went on and on and on, and I enjoyed it. It was vital; we couldn't afford to lose that match and we didn't."

It was not for nothing that he was nicknamed "Barnacle", and there was another famous stonewalling performance against the Australians in Brisbane in 1958. He was eventually bowled for 68, his innings lasting seven hours and 38 minutes. He scored off only 40 balls out of 426 he received. "We always lost in Brisbane, but personally I seemed to have quite a long innings there. In one of the long innings I had the satisfaction of hitting the most valuable six of all time, which is rather ironic. An Australian businessman offered £100 for the first six, and I of all people hit it. We had a magnificent party in Brisbane. It coincided with my birthday after the match. The following day those of us who weren't going on to Rockhampton made our way back to Melbourne, and we looked pretty rough. We walked into the foyer of the Melbourne hotel, and who should be coming out but Sir Robert Menzies, a marvellous man, a terrific speaker and a very fine politician. He looked at us and said, 'You boys could do with a grog,' so we went straight up to his suite and we had a couple of lagers each. He really was a cricket lover, who always made sure that when the Commonwealth had a meeting it always coincided with the Lord's Test."

That particular innings in Brisbane in 1958 was at that time the slowest 50 in first-class cricket, and it came in the country's first televised Test match. 357 minutes for 50, while his innings of 68 lasted for 458 minutes and he faced 427 balls. If nothing else, it was an amazing feat of concentration, although it would have done nothing for viewing figures. "One of the big snags is that the really good player, the Huttons and the Comptons, can play a slow innings and then go forward and change style. I could never do that once I got into the groove. My groove was to assume that every ball would be a good ball, and it was going to pitch middle and hit either the off or the leg, and my job was to keep it out. When a half-volley comes you don't expect it, at least I didn't. Originally I was considered to be a stroke maker, but when I got into the England side I used to go in number six, and we had a tail all of whom were quite capable of getting twenties or thirties or sometimes more. It seemed to me that if I stayed there until number 11 came in, then two of them might go cheaply but we would chip away at the runs and could put together quite a reasonable score. Normally with their attack, three of our good players went early and two would get 100, and the tail could assemble another 150 and then we were in with a good chance, because our attack was strong and well-balanced."

Bailey was an essential part of that attack, initially as a strike bowler, but did his bowling begin to take on the same aspects as his batting, namely steady and reliable? "I came into the side as an opening bowler. I was meant to be a fast bowler but I was never that quick, and then when Trueman and Statham, Tyson and Loader came on the scene I dropped into the role of third seamer, which I think I was more suited for. For Essex I always opened the bowling but for England, at a higher level, third seamer was the ideal situation."

Was the performance in Sabina Park, Jamaica, when he took seven first-innings wickets against the West Indies, the highlight of his bowling career for England? "Without a doubt, because no one expected it. We had to win the match to tie the series but our best bowler, Brian Statham, was injured and we thought, 'How are we going to win? Should we play Alan Moss, who was out there, or should we go in with three spinners?' We looked at the wicket, and it was a really glorious wicket. We had been practising for three or four days beforehand, and it glistened in the sun. We thought we'd only got one chance and that was to win the toss, score an awful lot of runs and then our spinners will bowl them out, so we went in with Fred Trueman and myself and three spinners.

"There was a look of horror on Len Hutton's face when he lost the toss, and we went out into the field. He asked me which end I would like. Fred was obviously quicker and an away swing bowler, as I was, so I said, 'Fred must have the crosswind to help the away swing and bowl with the wind, and I'll bowl into the wind and hope for the best.' The wickets kept tumbling, and I never understood why. If at the start of the innings you'd have said 'I'll give you 3 for 100,' I'd have said, 'Thank you very much indeed, I'll take that.' But that evening I was batting, so it was a remarkable day with no real reason. The ball moved a little bit, everything went right and if it went in the air it went to hand. It was one of those days."

Let alone taking 3 for 100, he took 7 for 34 in 16 overs to bowl out the West Indies for 139. Hutton scored 205, Bailey bagged another wicket in the second innings as the spinners went to work, and England won by nine wickets to level the series at two-all. Obviously that was a very enjoyable experience, but he gave the impression that touring in general was a pleasurable experience that suited him very well. "Touring was tremendous fun because we went out by ship, certainly to Australia and South Africa, and that was very pleasant. It was rather like living in a luxurious hotel with a swimming pool, and it was great fun. I used to imagine that I would be bored by the end, but it suited me; I liked it. Also, the press used to travel out with us and we used to get to know the press men very well. Not that you necessarily agreed with everything they wrote, but you got to know and understand them. I always remember Len saying one should never read the press unless you're doing well, which I always thought was the most sensible and so I followed that routine. If I had a good match I read it and loved it. If I had a bad match, and I knew more than anybody if I'd had a bad match, then I never bothered to read it. That was my philosophy throughout my life and it paid off."

These were the days of amateurs and professionals, and one way to circumnavigate the distinctions was to be an amateur cricketer but get paid for an administrative post. That is what Bailey did with Essex. "I was assistant secretary originally with Robert Patterson, and then Horace Clarke came in as an honorary secretary. Eventually I became secretary and I enjoyed it. It kept me amused. I think the luckiest thing was the whole time I took the minutes for the Essex County Cricket Club committee. I think we only had three disagreements the whole of the time I was there, which is remarkable because I was there for 20 years.

"One, which was the ironic one, was, I think, in 1948 or '49, when I went up to Worcester to find out how they had organised their football pool. I came back with all the details because we were ideal for a football pool, being a big county with lots of money to be made. I outlined everything to the committee, but they said that cricket couldn't be supported by gambling, so I lost that one. I think I got just one supporter, and that was Doug Insole.

"Life is so much luck, and the most satisfactory moment was when Worcestershire had won the Championship. I went up to the celebration dinner and ran into some friends from Warwickshire with whom I've always got on very well. They came up to me and asked how things were going. I said that there was only one trouble, we were short of money, which we always were. They asked, 'Is there anything we can do?' This was just before the dinner and I said, 'Lend us £13,000 interest-free and I can buy a cricket ground!' At the end of the dinner they came back and said, 'You can have it,' and that is why Essex are at Chelmsford now. It was as simple as that, and without that we couldn't afford the Chelmsford ground. We hadn't got any money and this interest-free loan from Warwickshire, for which I shall always be grateful, was the best thing I ever organised, because it gave us a ground for £13,000. We were in the red, and things went from strength to strength. If I hadn't gone to the dinner, if I hadn't met them and if they hadn't asked me, who knows? It was a great moment."

The spearhead of the bowling attack, being a leading batsman in the side, and he had administrative responsibilities as well. That really was getting back to the true all-rounder status. "I always had a very good assistant, and a very good girl who knew what was going on and when I forgot things reminded me. It was great fun. We had moments, and I always remember at Romford against Worcestershire we moved the boundary boards in, with their permission. We had batted the first day and they were going to have a shorter boundary, merely to get the crowd in. It was a lovely life, I enjoyed it."

And he had to organise the famous Essex circus going round from ground to ground. "I didn't do that so much, and fortunately I didn't have to move the stuff, but we had the ladies loo, which was an old bus, and we had our scoreboard, which was a removal van painted black with score information painted white on one side. It was great fun and again disappointingly, we would have loved to win the County Championship but we never really had a good enough side with sufficient balance. We had some very good cricketers, but we didn't have the spinners at one time, and another time we didn't have quite enough batting.

"I think actually we would have done very well in one-day cricket as it is played today, because we were the fastest-scoring side for a number of seasons. They used to have an award and I've got a couple of tankards. People get very upset when they see me with trophies for fast scoring. I have to admit that I didn't contribute that much to it, but again we had some great cricketers like Ray Smith, who was overworked. He used to open the bowling with fast-medium inswingers for about eight overs, then he'd put his cap on and bowl non-turning off-spinners. Then he'd take his cap off again and bowl inswingers again with the second new ball, and of course he hit the ball very hard.

"Peter Smith was a very good leg-break bowler and he featured in one of the great matches. He put on 218 for the last wicket against Derbyshire at Chesterfield in 1947 with Frank Vigar, and won the match. We had our moments but we lacked the consistency or a class attack like Surrey with Laker, Lock, Loader and Bedser. It was a different ball game and Yorkshire was another one we always had a hard game against. Trueman, Appleyard, Illingworth and Johnny Wardle, and always another seamer around as well. Their attacks were a different class."

It must have been a little dispiriting playing against the Yorkshires and Surreys, and playing with representatives of those counties in the England team. It could have made him envious of their domestic success while he had none with Essex. "You got used to it. We always started every season saying that we were going to go for the Championship, but by mid-June we realised that we weren't. I liked playing against the likes of Yorkshire and Surrey in particular.

"We had a very good record against Surrey, but Yorkshire tended to roll us over much too much, and it was years and years before I was on a winning side for Essex against Yorkshire. Mind you, when the victory eventually came it was very nice. We were always a little bit unpredictable. There was no question that we normally lacked a match-winning spin bowler. Peter Smith got more wickets for Essex than any other bowler, but he was a bowler who was going to take 5 for 120 when the opposition was scoring 340. Great bowling on a good wicket, but he wasn't going to get 5 for 10 on a sticky and win the match, because he was a wrist-spinner and a fairly slow wrist-spinner, as distinct from someone like Laker or Lock or Wardle. They would get on certain wickets and it was very difficult, fascinating to bat against but very difficult."

Perhaps the ultimate tribute to Bailey came from Fred Trueman, who once said of him: "That man was such a fighter he should have been a Yorkshireman." Perhaps one of the reasons why spinners did not flourish in Essex was the nature of the pitches, traditionally green and geared for the seamers. "They were, for a number of reasons. Primarily because I was secretary, but you have to remember we played on park wickets and if you took the grass off, it went, so you had to retain a wicket that was going to last for three days. What used to happen was that it would move on the first day and sometimes on the second day as well, and by the end it would get better and better, but if we removed the grass, the top would have gone and it would have been very dangerous. We tended to leave a certain amount of grass on, which obviously didn't help the spinners but the seamers enjoyed it.

"The wickets generally tended to get easier to bat on. Clacton was a ground that you couldn't understand. I could never work it out. If it moved in the morning, the afternoon was an absolute

All-rounder: with his fast-medium bowling and an obstinate batting technique, Bailey was an England regular for a decade and named Wisden Cricketer of the Year 1950

dream for batting. It was fast and true with good bounce and a fast outfield, if a little bit bumpy. Then round about 6.30 it would start greening up again, and you could see where the ball pitched. It was a fascinating ground, but I couldn't quite understand it."

One of the spinners who was fairly critical of the Essex pitches was Jim Laker, who went to play for Essex three years after he stopped playing for Surrey in 1959. "I talked Jim into coming on the way back from a dinner in Manchester. He said he might like to play cricket again as an amateur. Much to my surprise, some of my committee were against it. I couldn't understand it. Here we had the best spin bowler in the country for nothing for a few games, and it was going to do us a lot of good. The first over he bowled for us was at Ilford. He wasn't a great practiser and the press were saying he hadn't played for a long time, but he simply came on, it turned and lifted, and Gordon Barker dropped the batsman at backward short leg. It was absolute perfection; he was a great, great bowler. I remember there was a game at Romford, and I won the toss and asked Jim to go and have a look at the wicket, to decide whether we should have a bat or put them in. Jim departed and seemed to have been away for ages. When he returned I asked him where the hell he'd been and he replied, 'I've been looking for the wicket!'"

That was an example of a senior player Bailey recruited to the Essex ranks, but there were also a number of youngsters that he brought into the side who made a significant contribution to Essex cricket. "The most interesting thing about the job, really, was taking on the young players. We used to take them on normally about 15 or 16, sometimes older, and apart from four, you just didn't know. I did know you are taking a gamble, because some made it, some didn't. The nicest thing was taking them on, but the hardest thing I found by far was telling a player at the end of the season that he wasn't going to be retained. Some of them were quite convinced they were going to make it but I knew they weren't. I did find that very, very difficult.

"Of course, the good ones were pretty obvious and there was never any doubt. Barry Knight came down when he was 16, and at Chelmsford we used to have a knockabout in the middle. I put him in to play with another batsman, and it was the county side who were bowling at him. I saw him for 20 minutes and there was never any doubt. He was going to be a first-class cricketer, and given everything right he was going to be more than that; he was an international prospect without any doubt about it all. Then somebody said he bowled as well. I couldn't care less whether he bowled because he could make it as a batsman. He was a class player and he was a very, very fine all-round cricketer.

"Another one was Keith Fletcher, whom I heard about when he was 14. He was at a little school out in Cambridgeshire. A very intelligent careers officer went round and asked what the pupils wanted to do and this little boy, who was very small then, said he wanted to become a first-class cricketer. He then had a word with the headmaster, who wrote to Harry Crabtree and it came to me. I had a look at him and he was obviously very good indeed. I went up to Don Smith, a delightful man who used to run the young amateurs, and I said, 'I want to play this boy in the young amateurs team. He is only 14 but he's going to be very good indeed.' He wasn't very keen on the idea but he put him in, and he did the one thing for which there is no answer, he scored runs and completely won Don over.

"It was typical of Keith's brain as well when he was playing for the young amateurs against Middlesex, who were a pretty strong side. Keith was eventually joined by the number 11, who came on the staff later, and he went up to Don Smith and said, 'I've been joined by number 11, shall I give it a bit of tap now, sir?' He was fortunate in that he could bat at number six and let him just play the shots. In those days he was a very aggressive player. He used to hit the ball off the back foot over extra cover with a straight bat; a beautiful young player and the prospects were there.

"We used to get letters from people saying why don't you sign so-and-so, and I got a letter from a lieutenant who subsequently became a major-general. He said he had a very good cricketer called Barker, and I wrote back to ask whether he was qualified for Essex. Back came the answer, no, but he still thought I should look at him. He was going to be playing at Catterick on Sunday and we were playing at Hull. He suggested that as it was just down the road, why didn't I have a look at him?

"Hull is not just down the road from Catterick, it's a hell of a drive, but Doug Insole came with me and we watched Gordon Barker. He got some runs and I liked the look of him. We asked him to play against Canada at Clacton, and he came down and I shared a room with him. In the first innings he got nought, and he paced up and down the room all night long. It was a terrible night, but in the second innings he got a hundred and we said he could come on the staff.

"I think probably the most dramatic one was in Barbados. I was captaining a Rothmans Cavaliers side out there and we played the full Barbados side. Sobers, Griffiths and three or four others went off to play for the West Indies against Australia, so the next game we played was mainly their second XI. Opening their bowling was a man called Boyce, who was quick, and he then scored an electric 50, hitting the ball out of sight mainly with a cross bat, but he had a lovely eye and he was a beautiful fielder with a flat, fast throw. I've always believed if you're going to bring a player back to England, unless he's a star performer, he's got to be more than just a cricketer; he's got to be spectacular. I thought he was spectacular, so what more can you ask? A natural athlete, a fast bowler, a hard hitter and a marvellous fielder. And he was a very nice person, because I also checked on his background. That was Keith Boyce, and it wasn't a bad choice."

Bailey found Boyce in the West Indies, and he found Keith Fletcher, who went on to lead England, so was it a source of disappointment to him, even bitterness, that he never had the chance of captaining his country? "I would certainly like to have done that. It was one thing that I would certainly have liked to have done. I went out as vice-captain to the West Indies, but I was too young then. I think the ideal time for me to be captain was about 30. Everyone has regrets, but in the year when I got 2,000 runs and 100 wickets, which wasn't a bad performance, I think I might have got into the England side as an all-rounder, and we hadn't got one at that time. I think in that era I would have liked to have done it because it would have been very interesting. But I don't think I've ever felt bitter; it was just one of those things. I would have liked to have done it, obviously, but bitterness no, regrets yes."

One of the reasons given for the fact that Bailey was never appointed England captain relates to a book he wrote called Playing to Win *in 1954, following the tour to the West Indies in which he triumphed in Kingston. Was there any basis to that claim?* "There may well have been some truth in this, because you weren't allowed to write about the tour you had been on. I wrote a bit on West Indian cricket, but there was nothing in the book that anybody could have complained about, and a Sunday newspaper wanted to take some extracts. That was fine, but they wanted to have it slightly hotted up, so my brother, who was a journalist, did that for me. There was nothing in it and it was completely harmless. We were playing in Chalkwell Park, and on the Saturday morning I got what was the first article and it was nothing like what had been written. It was entirely different, and I phoned up the editor because I was worried. He said that I could go to London and change it, but I was just about to go out to play, so there was nothing I could do about it. It appeared as it was and they objected to it, but it wasn't my intention at all."

It was therefore somewhat ironic that when he gave up playing he should go into the journalism and broadcasting business. "Throughout my career I wrote. I wrote my first book in 1949, and articles non-stop. I was writing for the *Financial Times* at the end of my career on cricket and football, so I'd always be connected that way. And I enjoyed it."

Bearing in mind that he had experience as secretary of Essex, did he ever consider going into cricket administration at the end of his career? "When I finished with Essex I could have stayed on as secretary, and this was a big problem. Did I want to stay on for the rest of my life? Sometimes I think it was a pity I didn't and I wish I had done. On the other hand, I've had a very good life without doing that. It was tempting and the offer they made me was extremely generous by the standards of the time. What they were offering me was very good money for a secretary and far more than I would have got from the majority of counties. I thought about it and I was tempted, but I was involved in writing and one or two odds and ends, so I decided not to.

"Also there was the question of joining the committee, but having been secretary for 20-odd years I thought there was no possibility of going back on the committee, because whatever the secretary does I'd have thought, 'Oh dear me, I would never have done that,' so I thought I would cut adrift for ten years, and I don't know, life went on and I never bothered. I'd had a lot of fun doing it but I think that was the right moment to go."

He always kept closely involved with the county, and followed its fortunes very closely. He enjoyed the success, both on the field and financially, that started with the County Championship and Benson & Hedges Cup in 1979 and went on for a decade. That side was essentially the young team with which he left them. The success came at a time when the game changed, especially in international cricket when the West Indies ruled the world with their battery of fast bowlers. Was there any way it was a better game from the one he played? "From the spectators' point of view it was an infinitely worse game. I'm not talking about the one-day game, merely talking about the monotony of seeing four fast bowlers bowling a few overs per hour and no spinners. There's a sameness about it that I find extremely depressing.

"I always remember playing Nottinghamshire and we lost some wickets early, and I joined Gordon Barker. We batted through to lunch, and we faced their opening pair of bowlers, then we played their third and fourth bowlers, all right-arm seam bowlers. We came out after lunch and they started with their two openers, then their next two and then they brought on their fifth bowler, who was also a seamer. We came in at teatime and we were obviously quite happy because both of us had got runs, but I was bored so I thought the crowd must be terribly bored. The same field, the same shots, the same push, the same cut, Gordon produced the odd hook over after over, and the game without a spinner is a bit like bacon without any eggs."

In cricketing terms, Bailey needed the full English. That was evident as he gave his views of the game with great clarity and perception during his years as an expert summariser on Test Match Special. He also revealed a vibrant sense of humour that those who knew him had always appreciated, but which had not been evident in his batting. He was extremely popular in that role until he was dropped in 1999 along with Fred Trueman, but he continued to be acclaimed by his public. When a tribute lunch to celebrate his 80th birthday was organised, it required three sittings to accommodate all those who wanted to pay their respects. He died tragically in a fire in the flat to which he had moved from his long-time home in Westcliff, The Drive, an address which appealed to his sense of humour. He was 87, and Chelmsford Cathedral was packed for his memorial service. The order of service featured a photograph of Bailey, not playing a forward defensive or in any cricketing pose, but in full morning suit and top hat after receiving his CBE at Buckingham Palace. How fitting.

Cyril Washbrook
1914–1999

Cyril Washbrook

*M*ODERN CRICKET, IT IS *often said, lacks characters. Perhaps so, but there's no way that Lancashire cricket between 1933 and 1959 lacked character, because during that time, the county was fortunate enough to boast one of the great characters of English cricket in its ranks.*

Cyril Washbrook was born in Barrow, near Blackburn, in 1914, made his Lancashire debut at the age of 18, and in only his second match scored 152 against Surrey, at a time when massive scores were not commonplace. He went on to claim a place in the England team in 1937, only to have his Test career cruelly interrupted by the war. Even so he returned with two marvellous seasons in 1946 and '47, and became, with Len Hutton, a member of one of England's most successful opening partnerships. The mere sound of the names Hutton and Washbrook had a solid, comforting ring about it.

It appeared that his Test career had ended in 1951, but as a selector at the time, he came back in 1956 and marked his return with 98 against Australia at Headingley. He averaged 42.81 in his 37 Tests, with six centuries and 12 fifties. In all first-class cricket he scored over 34,000 runs, at an average of 42.67, with 76 centuries. He became Lancashire's first professional captain in 1954, and later became president of the club he served so well. It was sitting in the President's Room at Old Trafford that he recalled how he first became involved in the game.

"Well, I played one or two matches in the Ribblesdale league as a boy of about 11 or 12, for the village of Barrow, and I went on from there to continue playing club cricket. I moved from Barrow down to Bridgnorth in Shropshire, and I was at school there for six or seven years, and I played both for the town and for my grammar school at Bridgnorth. I scored a lot of runs, and as a result, three counties became interested in my performance. First of all it was Lancashire, and Worcestershire and Warwickshire were also interested, so I had to make a choice between the three, and naturally I came to the county of my birth, which I'm very proud to have played for, and been captain of, over the years. I was very well looked after when I played an odd match for Warwickshire second XI, a friendly match against Derbyshire, and they were very keen to sign me on, but I felt that I really belonged to Lancashire, and I'm very pleased that I did that."

He did not get the opportunity to watch Lancashire as a boy because he was living in the Midlands, but he did not watch much cricket near his home either. "I was about 28 miles from Worcester, and also from Warwickshire, and it was quite an effort to move about in those days, so therefore I didn't have the opportunity, and I didn't see Lancashire play until I came here in 1933, as a young man of 18 years of age."

He was playing club cricket, and presumably there were people in club cricket who had played first-class cricket? "No, not really. They were all good amateur cricketers. There were no professionals in the cricket that I played for the town of Bridgnorth, and of course the other cricket was played against grammar schools in the Midlands, so I saw practically nothing of first-class cricket until I reported here one day to come on the staff at Lancashire.

"I remember getting off the train at Warwick Road, and I didn't know very much about how to get on the ground. I saw an elderly gentleman with a cricket bag, and I said to him, 'Could you tell me how I get into the ground?' and he said, 'Well, I'm going there, you'd better come along with me.' He didn't say very much, but he said, 'Are you a batsman or a bowler?' so I said, 'I'm a batsman.' So he said, 'Well there's not much opportunity for batsmen here, it's more for bowlers.' It turned out to be the great Sydney Barnes, of many great performances in cricket, and he brought me on to the ground, and introduced me to the coach, Harry Makepeace, and said, 'This young man's come here to join the staff, you know about him more than I do.' That's how I began my journey through all the games, and miles and miles of cricket for Lancashire."

Did he face S.F. Barnes at all? "I played against him once, in a second XI match. He used to play for Staffordshire, and this was at Wigan. Of course he was then over 60 years of age I think, and he was still quite a good bowler. I didn't make many runs—I was out before he came on to bowl, so I didn't actually play against him as such at the other end of the 22 yards, no."

He did not get many runs that day, and resisted taking the opportunity to tell Barnes that he was the lad that the great man had shown to the ground at the outset of his career. "No, I didn't. He was obviously concentrating on the bowlers, and nothing happened after that until, when I scored my 152 against Surrey, he just came up to me and touched me on the shoulder, and pointed to the wicket out at Old Trafford and said, 'Well done.' That's all, he was a man of very few words actually, and not being a bowler, of course I didn't come under his coaching."

Who else was starting their careers about the time that he did, and who was on the staff at Old Trafford at that time? "Dick Pollard started the same day as I did on the staff here, and there were people like Eddie Phillipson also on the staff, Bill Farrimand used to keep wicket. We had some useful performers on the ground, and we played second XI cricket, and we used to have to pay attention when a first-class game was going on. We used to sit down with Harry Makepeace, and we'd talk about cricket, and it was all very interesting and I learned a lot from that.

"We practised hard at the nets, morning and afternoon. I'm talking about ground staff now, and of course the county cricketers did the same for about three weeks before the season started. We didn't do a lot of the physical exercises you see them doing today, we worked hard at playing cricket. For instance, I've never run round Old Trafford in my life, and you see people running round before the start of a match these days, and it always amuses me to think that I was here some, goodness knows how many years, and I never once ran round the ground. I got fit through playing cricket at the nets.

"And I was fit for cricket. I didn't break down very often, only about once in my career. I think I had a broken thumb, and I wasn't able to play first-class cricket for some little time as a result, but I never actually broke down, and had very few muscular troubles, and if I did they'd put a bit of plaster round it and that was it, and I went out and played. Today, there's so much physical preparation, and also physiotherapists, the room is full of all sorts of gadgets upstairs here, which we had never seen before. All we saw was just one table, and the youngsters couldn't get on there, because it may have been wanted for the first XI. We were in a very secondary position in the second XI, I mean you had to knock on the door to get into the dressing room of the first team in those days."

But it was a good way to learn cricket, because he was absorbing the atmosphere, and he was seeing what the game was all about, and gradually improving. "Yes, we came here to play cricket, and play cricket we did. There were club and ground matches on almost every day, and second XI cricket. It wasn't the case that if you weren't in the county side, you wouldn't be playing. You were playing all the time, and that's the way to get fit, and that's the way to play cricket, and learn how cricket is done in all means of playing."

Despite the fact that he never lapped Old Trafford and did not indulge in too much physical preparation, he was renowned as an outstanding fielder, one of the great cover points in the game at the time. "Yes, I enjoyed fielding, and it gave me a lot of pleasure to move about quickly, pick up the ball, and bang it in to the wicket-keeper, those were days I quite enjoyed. Some people don't enjoy fielding, but I did, I thoroughly enjoyed it. Batsmen are often very good fielders, and bowlers are often limited in batting. No, I think it's something that you've got to like or not. Some people like fielding. I liked it. I just played my club and ground matches, or second XI or first-class matches, fielded at cover point, and that's how my reputation grew, I suppose."

There must have been individuals who were influential in starting him off in the game. Who coached him, or were there any players that he watched, and admired, and tried to model himself on? "On the staff I saw a lot of first-class cricket; I mean as soon as we finished our practice at the nets, we had to come and sit down and watch the game, as a ritual. We had our lunch, practised at the nets for quite a long period, and then came back to the pavilion again to watch the game, and that's how we began to learn about it.

"I was always a great admirer of J.B. Hobbs, and I saw his last century scored here at Old Trafford in George Duckworth's benefit match, way back I suppose in about 1933 or '34, and he was my schoolboy idol. There were other people I had great admiration for, people like Wally Hammond, who I think was the greatest cricketer I've ever seen, and I enjoyed watching and listening to people talking about cricket. When I first began playing first-class cricket, when we were on tour down in the south or wherever it was, I used to listen to these older people talking about the game. They did talk about it in those days; they didn't take off their flannels at half past six and forget about it, they really indulged in great conversation. I learned an awful lot, and about half past ten at night I was sent off to bed, you know, 'Get up them stairs,' sort of thing, and it did me an awful lot of good."

What about the Lancashire players that he remembered of that era? "Ernest Tyldesley was a great player. He scored 100 centuries for Lancashire, something like that, and I think he was about the best player in the Lancashire team that I played with in my early stages. He was still a fine cricketer in his forties, and a gentleman as well."

There was a great tradition in Lancashire. A lot of the place was built on a tradition of playing the game properly, and playing winning cricket. "Oh yes, that's very true. We went out to win every game we played, and there was a great deal of thought put into who was to bowl at whom, and how to bat against certain bowlers, and you learned a lot watching and talking to these players. That's how I learned about cricket, watching and talking to players who'd played in the first-class game."

His first-class debut came in 1933. "I played against Sussex at Old Trafford. I think I made about seven in the first innings and 40 not out in the second innings, and I played for the first time against the great fast-medium bowler Maurice Tate, who I think was the greatest of his type that I ever played against. Don't forget, he was nearing the end of his career when I started to play, and he was still a great bowler. He had mastery of movement and control, and he hit the pitch so hard, and he came off the wicket very quickly, you had to be halfway forward and ready to play, and he did move the ball late."

He was nearly 18, when he arrived at Old Trafford, and had not seen that much first-class cricket. Did anything about the game surprise him? "I think it was full of minor surprises, how people prepared themselves to bat, what the bowlers did, what they used to eat at lunchtime. If they were bowling they didn't eat anything except a sandwich or something like that. They didn't have a big meal, and all these things you learn by observation really, how they conduct themselves, and then you try to fit your way of life into the mode of life that they lived."

As very much a junior in the side, was he put upon and expected to know his place in the pecking order? "Well, I was very much a junior, but I had great respect for them and I never had any bother at all with any member of the side. The only thing was that my bedtime was about half past ten at night—'Get up them stairs!' But I realised that it was all to my benefit to do these things, because I wanted to succeed."

Did he ever have any doubts that he might not succeed? "Cricketers have good times and bad times, and especially when you're beginning cricket, you have quite a number of failures, and I think you've got to learn to accept failures as well as success. One got a lot of encouragement from the senior players in the side in those days, they were all helpful, and I enjoyed it very much. I suppose I began to succeed as a batsman, really, in the third season I was at Old Trafford.

"1936 was the beginning of me being a regular member of the side, and I had a certain amount of success, and in 1937 I played my first Test match, for England against New Zealand at the Oval. I didn't do very well, but at least I'd walked on the field, and got an England cap, and that I was terribly proud of."

How did winning an England cap compare with getting his Lancashire cap? "They were both great moments in your career. I was given my county cap in 1933, and it was presented to me by the then president, as they did in those days, in the committee room, and the usual speech was, 'We hope you'll uphold the traditions of Lancashire cricket, both on and off the field.' Those words stuck in my memory, and I suppose I tried to live up to them."

His England debut came in 1937 when he was were still only 22. Was there a big jump between county cricket and Test cricket? "The touring side in that year was New Zealand, and I got in because Eddie Paynter was unfit. He had been a great player, and he received an injury, and I must have been put down as one of the players in case of injury to the original selection. If you pick an England side, obviously you've got to pick people you must be able to call upon at a moment's notice if anybody is injured, and I must have been one of the players that were in reserve, and as a result of Eddie Paynter not being fit I played my first Test match. There was no inkling given to me that if you do well in such and such a match, you'll be in the England side, nothing like that happened at all. I was just anxious for a place."

Who did he find himself in a Test dressing room with? "Denis Compton was also playing in his first Test match. Walter Robins was the captain; Charlie Barnett was playing for England at the time. I can't think of the side completely, but there were Joe Hardstaff and people like that, all very, very fine players, and I was given my England cap by Sir Pelham Warner in the dressing room at the Oval. That was a very proud moment for me."

Batting at number three in the first innings Washbrook scored nine, but he managed eight not out in the second innings. "I opened in the second innings because there was only about half an hour to go and Len Hutton had to make a long journey up to Scarborough or something, and it was about 5.30, and he had a train at 6.30, and I was told to go in at number one with Charlie Barnett. It was a drawn match, bad weather and so on."

So he was not always an opener? "Not always, no, but I made my reputation as an opener. When I played for Lancashire in the early stages, I went in about number five, number six, and then gradually as time went on I got the opportunity of opening the innings. When Frank Watson retired, about a year after I came here, that gave the opportunity to some young player to open the innings, and I took it, I hope."

He was well equipped for that, because he was particularly good off the back foot, cutting and hooking. "Yes, well all good players are good back players. Today there's too much forward defensive push, which to my mind is quite ridiculous. All the best players have a lot more time to play the ball than the modern performers, and therefore they have time to play back, and the other chappies push to play forward."

He was at that time earmarked as being one of the England players of the future, and then the war came and interrupted his career. "I was in the Air Force for five or six years, whatever it was. I used to play for the RAF against the Army, and fortunately I was stationed at the RAF College in Cranwell, which was a place that was ready made for sport. It was like the Sandhurst of the RAF, they were good wickets to play on, and we had a lot of fun playing, a great relief from the normal routine of being in the Air Force."

He put the facilities to good use, managing to play quite a lot of cricket during the war. "Well, one-day matches. Army v. Air Force and things like that, all for charity you know. I played quite a few games at Lord's, and played an odd game at Old Trafford as well, but basically there wasn't a lot of cricket to be played during those six years."

But the standard, and people he was playing with and against, was presumably fairly high. "I wouldn't say it was high, but I had the good fortune, as I say, to play quite a few games. It wasn't called first-class cricket, because they were only day matches. The CO never refused to give me permission; once you were invited to play for the Air Force it was automatic that you got away. I remember once when the war was nearly over, and a lot of matches were being arranged throughout the country by the RAF. I had a letter from the officer responsible for the Air Force side with a string of matches, day after day, so I went to my CO and said, 'I've got an invitation to play in these matches, so could I have leave?' So he said, 'Well, I can't give you leave, but I can give you a paper to say, "This person has permission to be playing cricket in these matches." It's not leave; you're still in the Air Force.' He wasn't a cricketer, but he couldn't say no, because it came from way up high, and that's how I played in 1945. We played a lot of cricket that summer. I was still in uniform, still supposed to be at my station, you know, but it was a lot of fun. We were responsible, I suppose, for getting people interested in the game immediately after the war. That was the intention, or the first intention was to raise money for charity, which we did, because crowds came in very large numbers to watch us play, at Lord's and Old Trafford and places like that, and it was a lot of fun."

It was said that he was one of those players who were particularly affected in his career by the war years. Did he look back with any feelings that he was robbed of what might have been the best years of his career? "Well, not really. I suppose I was on the verge of playing more international cricket. I only played once in '37, but I was fortunate in this respect, that I did play these matches which basically were for charity, but there were also some very good cricketers playing in them, from the Army and the Air Force, mainly. They helped me develop my career. I was playing in fairly high class cricket, you see, not deserting the game for five or six years. I did play quite a bit."

He came back to Lancashire in 1946 and 1947, and had wonderful summers, with 2,000 runs in each of them, averaging 68 a time. "Fortunately they were fairly good summers. We had some decent wickets to play on, and obviously five years in the career of, say, a fast bowler who was doing very well before the war, he's not quite as good after five years. I suppose that the bowling in particular wasn't quite as good as before the war, when we started to play in '46, '47. Obviously they'd got a couple of years to learn how to play, many of them, learn how to bowl, and set fields, attacking fields and defensive fields and so on, according to the state of the wicket, and these chaps had to settle in. Fortunately I played before the war, and settled in pretty quickly when we came back to civilian life.

"Obviously six years in a batsman's life is very considerable, but it doesn't affect him so much as a fast bowler, who is probably finished by the time six years have gone by, and then the younger bowlers have got to come on and learn how to bowl according to the field that is placed, and naturally experienced batsmen were able to cash in on that sort of thing."

What changes were there at Old Trafford when he came back after the war? "Obviously one or two players had retired. But we still had Harry Makepeace to coach us after the war, and it settled down into a routine that was almost identical with pre-war days. The playing staff was naturally quite young, and they had a lot to learn, and it took a little time to get them into the first-class routine."

From 1946 to 1951 he was a regular in the England side, and he had as his opening partner Len Hutton for most of the time. It was a stable, established opening partnership that was immensely

Legendary pairing: Hutton and Washbrook (r) coming out to bat in the Trent Bridge Test of 1948

successful. "I think it was successful. We both played our own game, he didn't tell me how to play, and I never made any suggestions to him how he should play either. We had a good understanding in running between the wickets; I think we were only run out once in the whole of the years we played together. That was when Len fell down in South Africa, in Cape Town, that was the only time there was ever any trouble with running between the wickets. That helps a lot, because if you're moving your score along, it always gives you confidence to have a partner who is prepared, and can run between the wickets. I was lucky with Lancashire, having Eddie Paynter as an opening batsman with me, he was a great runner between the wickets, and your score is never docile, it's always on the move, and that's a great help. It comes naturally, I think. You have confidence in the chap who's at the other end, in his judgement, so it progresses."

How did he rate Len Hutton as a batsman? "He was a very great batsman, one of the greatest. I enjoyed batting with him. He had a very serious approach to cricket, and we just had great confidence, I think, in the other's performance. Of course he was responsible for creating many records in cricket. I didn't think he'd always got them at the back of his mind, but I remember walking down the pavilion steps in Johannesburg in South Africa in the 1948/49 tour, and we'd been in since the beginning of the day. As we walked down the steps to go on to the field, some chap leaned over and said, 'You want 24 to beat the record.' So Len said to me, 'What record is that?' I said, 'I don't know,' and he said, 'I don't either, but we'd better just see that we get them.' And we did, of course."

It was a partnership of 359 and took only 310 minutes. "Did it? Well I know it came just after tea anyway, at Ellis Park in Johannesburg, and it just shows the confidence we had in each other's ability."

It is a record opening partnership for England still standing well into the 21st century, and it was a partnership in which runs came at quite a rate. "Yes, it's quite a good rate. It was a very good wicket, I must say that. We got on with the scoring because we played our strokes and enjoyed it."

Washbrook also shared a mammoth opening partnership with Winston Place, putting on an unbroken 350 against Sussex at Old Trafford in 1947, before rain forced a declaration when they were in sight of the record opening partnership for Lancashire of 368, compiled by Archie MacLaren and Dick Spooner in 1903. "I'm not really record-conscious, but Winston Place was a successful player as an opening batsman, and I enjoyed playing with him. He was a very good player."

He might not have been a records man, but there was no way he could be described as anything else than a serious-minded cricketer, just as he described Len Hutton. "I always took a serious view of the game, yes. I always thought I had certain responsibilities, and tried to carry them out. I think there wasn't very much difference in our actual approach to the game. He was a greater player than I was, but I enjoyed batting with him. He was a good back player, with plenty of time to play the ball, and that's the secret of being a good batsman, it's how much time you have to play."

So the two of them were serious-minded because there was not any room for frivolity when it came to the game, but there was still enjoyment in it. "Oh yes, we had a lot of enjoyment playing cricket. I enjoyed it for years, even from the very start, when I had to do as I was told. I learned from these things and it was a great pleasure to play at any time for Lancashire. They had a serious-minded approach, a similar approach to the Yorkshire side in those days, and we had a reputation to uphold, and we did the best we could."

In 1954 he became Lancashire's first appointed professional captain. How much did that mean to him? "I was very proud to be given the honour of captaining Lancashire. I think it affected my play somewhat, because I began to go in a little bit lower down the order. We were either going well when I went in, wanting runs quickly, or we were in the cart, and I had to get my head down and play. Therefore it probably had a detrimental effect on the amount of runs I scored, because always I must give the example of playing for the side and not for myself."

How did other counties who still had amateur captains react to playing against his Lancashire side? "Oh, very well, there's always been a good spirit in cricket whether amateur or professional, and there's no detriment to the game, I don't think, that the odd county had a professional captain. I hope not, anyway."

Was he disappointed that he failed to bring the Championship to Old Trafford in that time? "Oh, yes, I was. We were rebuilding the side, really, and we did reasonably well in one or two seasons in which we played, but never actually won it. We were in very close competition with Surrey in one year, I can't remember which year it was, but rain prevented a result in the match and that was the end of it, we couldn't make the Championship side. The side was beginning to be very good. We'd got a number of young players with experience then, and as time goes on they become more and more experienced, and obviously it builds into a very good side. The senior people were people like Winston Place, Dick Pollard and John Ikin. Four or five senior players were able to help the younger players when they were coming into the side. We had a very good coach in Harry Makepeace at the time, and that makes a lot of difference to a county side, I think."

Because someone like that is ideal to bring young players through, and develop them, and make them capable of commanding first-team places? "Yes, after all, he was a double international. He played football for England, and also played cricket for England, and a very nice chap, a chap with a sense of humour but also a very senior approach to the game."

It looked as if, after a poor tour to Australia and New Zealand, that his Test career had come to an end in 1951. Was that the way he saw it? "I thought it was very near the end, as I didn't have a very good tour on that occasion. But don't forget that Australia were a very good side. Lindwall and Miller and these people were not pushovers. There were great players, great bowlers.

"We took one or two players out there that were not actually, I think, quite ready to play in a Test match against Australia. I think that the side that came to England in 1948, for instance, was the greatest side that's ever played for Australia. Don Bradman thought it was; he of course was nearing the end of his career. They had everything that the game requires, fast bowling, medium pace, spinners, great batsmen, and a fine fielding side, and they were, in my opinion, the greatest side that I've ever seen. Other people much older than I am who saw sides before that time also think so. They were a truly great side; they'd got everything the game requires."

Touring is obviously more enjoyable when results are favourable, but did he generally enjoy touring? "Oh yes, I enjoyed touring. I enjoyed going about the world and seeing lots of places, and playing on grounds that I'd only read about as a young man. You get a very good team spirit in a touring side, which is sometimes difficult in England. The most enjoyable tour I think I went on was to South Africa. We had a very successful side; we had a very good captain in George Mann. He wasn't a great player himself but he was certainly a very good captain, he got the best out of everybody, and we had a very happy tour."

Washbrook became a Test selector while he was still captaining Lancashire. Was there any problem in combining the two duties? "Well, you had a certain amount of travelling about to do. To go and select sides on Saturday night, if you were playing in Manchester, you would have to get to London some way. We had a very good chairman in G.O. Allen, and it was a new experience which I thoroughly enjoyed."

It was in 1956, when he had been out of Test cricket for very nearly five years, that he was a selector and recalled to the side. "The selectors did that. We got to a certain stage in the meeting, having a certain amount of difficulty with odd places in the team, and Gubby Allen, who was the chairman, said, 'Well, we're going to talk about you now, so you'd better leave the room and order the beer!' So I said, 'Well, I don't think it's as serious as all that.' We'd lost against Australia at Lord's, with one or two failures in the side. So I was not kicked out of the room, but asked to leave, to go and order the beer, and come back in about half an hour or so. When I got back, Gubby Allen said, 'Well, we want you to play at Leeds. Will you play?' So I said, 'Well, you don't refuse to play for England. I still think it's not quite as bad as all that, but I'm very happy to play,' and that's how I came to be playing at Leeds in 1956. I didn't select myself; it was the other selectors who asked me if I would play."

He had few misgivings about taking up the challenge, and promptly went to Leeds and scored 98. "When I went in to bat,

England were 17 for three, and I shall remember that score to my dying day. Fortunately, at the other end batting with me, was that great player, Peter May, and we gradually got on top and we made a great success of it. He got out just before the end of the day. I was still there, but I had a wonderful reception from the Yorkshire crowd, going out to bat in the first place, and a great reception when I came back. I might have been a Yorkshireman! They were truly great, it was honestly the finest reception I've ever had."

He finished just two short of what would have been a fairy tale century. He claimed he did not have one eye on the scoreboard, and that he was satisfied to get 98. Perhaps he got a little apprehensive? "No, well I would have been pleased to get two more, but I can't imagine that I was ever very concerned about the fact. I'd been there nearly all day, and the point is, when you've batted that long, you don't care who bowls at you from the other end."

Was the LBW decision a good one? "Well, the umpire saw, so I'm quite satisfied, really."

He played through the rest of the series, but without success. "Oh no, I didn't do very well at Old Trafford, nor at the Oval in the final one."

But he went on playing for Lancashire until 1959 when he decided to retire. "I think there comes a time in your career when you think that you've had enough, and that it's becoming more of a strain and a struggle to play six days a week. It's hard work, you know, playing cricket six days a week when you're 40-odd years of age. I didn't want to go down the ladder, and not be regarded as a reasonable player, so I got out whilst I was still what I'd call a reasonable player, anyway."

Washbrook batting for Lancashire against Surrey at the Oval, 1958

But just as he came back to Test cricket, he had one more first-class match to come in 1964. "That was MCC v. Lancashire. I captained the MCC side. I was very pleased to do that, it was a great honour for the MCC to ask me to captain the side, which I did willingly."

Opening the batting, he scored 85 in the first innings and in the process passed 34,000 first-class runs. And that at the age of very nearly 50. How closely did he stay involved in the game after his retirement from playing? "Well, after about 12 months, things weren't going very well and they wanted to appoint a manager. After discussion, I allowed my name to go forward, and they appointed me as manager of the side. It only lasted about a year, and I didn't really enjoy it so much as playing. The side didn't do particularly well, we were struggling very badly, and I was really glad to get out of it. About two years after that I was voted onto the committee."

Washbrook therefore became one of the first cricket managers in the game, but for a variety of reasons it was not a particularly successful appointment. He believed that the captain was the key man, not the manager. Did he enjoy being captain himself? "Yes, I quite enjoyed it. We had reasonable success. I suppose it mustn't be very good if you're captain of a very ordinary side, but I was fortunate that it wasn't the case. We just weren't quite good enough to come right to the top."

Did he have ambitions to captain England at any time? "None whatsoever. I was very fortunate in the days of my captaincy that I had one of the greatest fast bowlers that's probably ever played for Lancashire, and that was Brian Statham. He was the easiest man in the world to manage. You'd say to Brian, 'Bowl that end.' He'd say, 'Yes, OK, skipper.' And if you'd say, 'Put your sweater on, Brian,' he did, without any trouble. You can often see little differences that occur on the field, but we never had a single moment of difference. If I asked him to bowl, he bowled, if I asked him to come off, he came off. He was a great, accurate bowler. He bowled straight, and always on the wickets, and naturally he's been a great bowler for England as well as Lancashire. You couldn't wish to have a better bowler to handle. He was truly marvellous in that respect, because fast bowlers are inclined to be a bit temperamental, and want to bowl sometimes but not others, but he was always the same."

Just as he returned to play Test and first-class cricket, he also returned to selectorial duties in 1971 and 1972. "I only did a short second period, but my most interesting time was the first. That's when I enjoyed it, perhaps because we had better players to choose from. It becomes hard work when you're searching the whole country for players who are fit to play for England. I certainly enjoyed the first period far better than the second one."

It is interesting to know how a Test team was actually selected. Did everybody write the names down that they thought should be playing, and then see what common ground there was, or how did it work? "No, it's thrown open to discussion. There are obviously certain people who are going to play. Then the problems come in fitting the rest in around the five or six certainties. Then you've got to build around that particular group, and make your selections accordingly. There was no real serious argument. Some polite discussions, but no roughness about it at all. It's a very pleasant job, really. It's a difficult job, it's very interesting, but you can't win. If you pick a side that wins, they're good cricketers, but if you're picking a losing side, the selectors are in trouble from the press. You can't stop people expressing their opinions; they're entitled to do so."

Even after his tenure of the cricket manager's position at Old

Trafford came to an end, Washbrook kept closely involved with the club by being elected to the committee by the members. Then, in 1989, he had the honour of being made president of Lancashire. "Yes, that came as a complete surprise to me. It was a great honour, and one which I accepted, and I quite enjoyed doing it. It's a lot of work to do, always attending committee meetings and things like that, but I must say that I've enjoyed it."

And as president, did he feel a responsibility to maintain the long-held traditions of the club? "Oh yes, to do your very best to see that things work out properly. I'm particularly interested in the actual playing of the game, more than other sections of the presidency."

Washbrook was no doubt as forthright in the committee room as he was on the field. He had a reputation for being somewhat aloof and forbidding, but that was perhaps a front to mask a basic shyness. He was the ultimate professional in the very best sense of the word. Never one to shirk a challenge, he tended to take on the quick bowlers when they banged them in short to him, and as an opening batsman he faced plenty of balls flying round his ears. "No, I never did much ducking and weaving when I was playing. If they bowled it short, I accepted the challenge, and I always used to get what I called inside the line of the ball, and it went over my left shoulder if I didn't connect."

Did he ever get hit? "Yes, I saw a recent film. I was hit on the head by Miller in this particular match. I'd forgotten all about it, but I saw it only a few days ago. It was the only time I was ever hit, yes, seriously. You can see a white mark where I had two stitches put in from Freddie Trueman in one Lancashire and Yorkshire match. But considering the amount of fast bowling I played against, the amount of times I've been hit is very, very few."

Cyril Washbrook enjoyed a wonderful career, from the time he was shown to Old Trafford from the Warwick Road station by the great Sidney Barnes, right through to becoming a record holding opening batsman for England. He played exactly 500 first-class matches for his beloved county and was awarded the CBE, somewhat belatedly, in 1991. He died eight years later at the age of 84.

Alec Bedser (r)
1918–2010, with his twin brother, Eric

Alec Bedser

*I*T'S A CRICKETING FACT *that Test-playing countries are noted for a particular type of bowler they produce. Mention the West Indies and Australia, and you think of the great fast bowlers; the sub-continent is noted for its spinners, and English success in Test cricket has invariably been founded on fast-medium bowlers who have the ability to swing the ball and gain movement off the seam. In this category there has been none better than Alec Victor Bedser. Alec Bedser was born in Reading, Berkshire, in 1918, was 21 when he made his debut for Surrey, and had developed into a bowling legend by the time he retired in 1960.*

Tall, powerful and with immaculate control, he played in 485 matches and took 1,924 wickets at just a fraction above 20 each. He bowled 106,192 deliveries. Just think about it. He played for England in 51 Test matches, taking 236 wickets at under 25 each, and not for him the cheap wickets while batsmen ducked the sheer pace at the other end. For eight years after the war he was the absolute mainstay of the England attack. There was little support for him. Appointed an England selector in 1962, he chaired the selectors from 1969 to 1981, managed two tours to Australia, and was assistant manager on another. He was made president of Surrey in 1987 and was honoured with a CBE for services to cricket. In 1996 he was knighted, with then prime minister John Major thought to have a direct influence in ensuring that Bedser's contribution to the game was suitably rewarded. There have been few who have given better service to English cricket.

Yet the great bowler who was Alec Bedser might never have emerged had it not been for the toss of a coin. The story goes that he and his twin brother Eric could not decide who was going to fulfil which role in the game. "Well, we both bowled the same, Eric and I. I bowled inswingers, he bowled outswingers, naturally. At about 16 to 17 we wanted to play in the same side, and Allan Peach, who ran the indoor school in Woking, said that if you want to get in the same side, one had better bowl differently from the other. And seeing Eric was an outswinger, which was a natural off-spin action, we decided that he would try to bowl off-spinners, which is what he did."

So where did the story of the toss of the coin come from? "I think we just said it to get over the thing quickly. People kept asking, so we said we tossed up for it. I think that's how it came about."

Whenever Alec Bedser was questioned about his early life in cricket, the answer was always in the plural, because his life was spent as one of identical twins. So, when asked how he started playing cricket in the first place, he replied: "We played when we were kids on a rough piece of ground with no proper facilities at all. We had one bat between about 40 of us, don't know whose bat it was, but we couldn't afford a bat until I was about 17, so we all mucked in and played on literally a piece of dirt that we used to sweep the stones off with a broom.

"That was until I was about 14 or 15, when we both joined Woking cricket club, which was really the first time we played on grass. I didn't play any real cricket at school at all, we used to play a lot amongst ourselves, pick up sides on the common after school, and on Saturdays and Sundays, but there was no organised cricket as such at school. Maybe two matches a year, which was a token sort of thing. We always wanted to play of course, and always had the ability to do it and play football, and then we joined the Woking cricket club and played for the second XI, and just worked hard really."

Did their father play cricket at all? "Dad played local cricket, for a club called Woodham which was near where we lived, and he was a part-time professional soccer player for Reading. He was keen on sport, but of course like everyone in those days he had to work, he didn't have much time for sport. He was a bricklayer, and often worked six days a week, so there wasn't much time for that, but he encouraged us. He didn't fuss about it or anything, and didn't come running around the matches we played, he always kept out of the way but was obviously very thrilled when we did all right."

With his father playing football at a high standard, did he have any ambitions on the football field? "Oh yes, Eric and I used to play right and left back, and both played for Woking schools and Surrey schools, and had a trial for England boys. We were asked to go and have a trial for Reading actually, when I was about 16, but we were working and couldn't go away, so that was it. I'm glad in a way that we didn't, because we became professional cricketers, and I think probably if I'd played football it might have messed my knees up, and I wouldn't have been able to do what I did on the cricket field."

When did he first get an inkling that he might be good enough to play cricket professionally? "We never did really, I don't think. I never thought I'd be good enough. It just gradually evolved really, I think through sheer hard work. We obviously had the ability, I mean the first time I picked a new ball up I swung it, so we knew that, and then we went to the indoor cricket school and old Allan Peach encouraged us, and he must have thought we had something about us, because he became coach at the Oval in 1936 or '37 I think it was, and he recommended us for a trial with Surrey. By then we were playing club cricket for Woking, and playing against men and getting them out and getting runs, so obviously we could play a bit, otherwise we wouldn't have done that, and from there it progressed."

He said that when he first bowled with a new ball, he found he could swing it, but did he remember when that was? "When I was about 16, the ball swung. I didn't know why and didn't know how, it was obviously the action, the same as Eric swung it away. What I remember mostly was playing for Woking against East Molesey when I was about 17, and they were a good side. R.W.V. Robins was playing for them, and they said I'd better bowl with the new ball and I did, and it swung like a boomerang, and I got six or seven wickets I think. That was the first time I played in a match and really remember seeing the thing swing. Getting wickets, I thought that was good."

This ability to take wickets resulted in the trial at the Oval. Did he remember much about that? "We played a year before. They used to have what they call the Surrey villages matches here, East v. West Surrey villages, and Alan got us to play in that, and then we played in a trial game. So we came straight off the indoor school, not having been on the turf at all, and came up and played in this match and Eric got a hundred in it. I don't think I got many wickets, but Allan Peach was here and they offered us terms to come on the staff, that was in 1938."

And who was around at the Oval at that time? "The first-team players were Alf Gover, Bob Gregory, Laurie Fishlock, Tom Barling, Stan Squires, all those names. They were very good when we arrived, very kind. Different days then to now. You weren't allowed in the pavilion at all, as employees of the club.

We used to walk round the back of the Oval, and the dressing rooms were down at the bottom. The pros were in one room and the amateurs changed upstairs. The junior pros changed at one level, and capped players were at the top level in the main dressing room. And we as young players weren't allowed to sit out on the balcony to watch the play, we had to go upstairs into the stand because we weren't first XI players. We didn't see anything wrong with that, and thought that the only way to sit on that balcony was to become a first XI player, and that was it, no one felt it was wrong. It was the same in that we had amateurs and professionals in different dressing rooms. No one thought it was wrong, or funny, we just got on with it. It's something that I think is lacking today a little bit. It seems to me too often that unless you make a fuss of people and pat them on the back they say they are not being encouraged, and I can't understand that. It was enough for me to get out there and play, that's what I wanted to do."

How much first-class cricket had he seen before he came to the Oval? "Not very much, we couldn't afford it of course. I only went to Lord's once, when we were in Woodham church choir, and the vicar was mad on cricket and he took Eric and me to see England v. India, the first Test match in 1932. The next time I went to Lord's was also England v. India and I played in it, which was quite a coincidence. Then we saw two games at the Oval until I was about 17. We would take our holiday, look at the fixture list and see who was playing at the Oval, and try to see Wally Hammond; come to the Oval and watch the cricket, that was our holiday."

He had commented that the other professionals were very kind to him when he arrived at the Oval. Did he get very much help and advice from them? "They'd give you tips if they thought you were doing something, but there was no such thing as coaching as such. Basically I think it was thought that if you were good enough to come on the staff, you're there and you picked it up by practice. Really it was the amount of practice and work you did, because you weren't selected to come on the staff unless you had some ability. So looking back I'm sure we used to put in an enormous amount of hard work in the nets, hours on end. We'd start nets here at quarter to 11, and bowl to the first team until quarter to one, and then from two o'clock until four we'd practice ourselves, and then from half past four until seven we'd bowl to members. If you were a member of Surrey you were entitled to 20 minutes in the nets, and you could ring up and say, 'I'm coming at, say, six o'clock, can I have two bowlers?' and we would be there ready, and the whistle would go, and 'Two bowlers please!' and we'd walk out and bowl to you for 20 minutes, and that's how we did it, hour after hour, we did that for two years, up to the war of course."

Would he bowl flat out at those members? "No, only if someone didn't give us a decent tip. Sometimes there were one or two mingy ones. You used to get sixpence basically, and if they didn't give you anything then we would bowl a little bit harder. We had a fellow named Major C.H.B. Pridham. He used to write in *The Cricketer*, he was one of these real old-fashioned chaps. He wore cane pads and an I Zingari cap, and he always used to come at twenty to seven, for the last 20 minutes. We had to stay, and he couldn't play, he was about 50 then. He only gave us sixpence, so we thought, we didn't want any more of that. He came one night and we'd had enough of him, so we put him in a rough net and bowled as fast as we could, and he stayed in for about three minutes and walked out and never came back! He went to Lord's for his net after that."

Major Pridham was not a bad judge! Bedser developed in the second XI fairly swiftly because it was not too long before he was making his Surrey debut, in 1939. "This brings home a point which, when we were talking about players, as I'm on the committee here at the Oval, and they say, 'He's promising, he's got a good action,' so I always say, 'How many people does he get out?' It's no good unless you can get people out at a lower level. I came here in '38 and played for the second team, and was top of the averages. I got 51 wickets at 16, and the next year I did the same thing, which proved I could bowl. They weren't just saying I had a good action, I was getting people out. Then I was given the chance and played against Oxford. I didn't do any good, and then the war came."

He did not do any good in that game against Oxford University, and neither did Eric, who was also making his first-class debut. They played against Cambridge University a week later and while Eric did take a wicket, Alec failed to do so despite the fact that Allan Peach was umpiring! It was not until 1946 that Alec claimed his first wicket, when in the second innings of MCC v. Surrey that he eventually struck, taking 6 for 14 in 9 overs. It illustrated how the war came as a serious interruption to his career, to his ambitions and to his hopes. "When you read all these things about statistics, having beaten this record and beaten that record, people forget that there were six years that you didn't play. It didn't matter about me, but what about Len Hutton and Denis Compton and all these people? I was just 21. I came back at 27. I didn't play cricket for three and a half years. I went to Italy, North Africa and everywhere else, went to France first in '39 with the BEF. Eric and I were together all the war, went to France in 1939, came back from Dunkirk, and then went out to North Africa in 1942 and came back in '46. Three years away, didn't play cricket at all. I think that was a good thing in a lot of ways, from 24 to 27, and we obviously did plenty of physical exercise, which you had to do. But what I think happened—and I've talked to specialists about this—in those years, all your sinews and ligaments became strong. You stop growing and everything else, and then when I came back to actually play I didn't break down, because by then I think you're fully developed and your body could withstand the strain that bowling is."

He was known for his stamina and it was said that he left the field only once during a first-class game, and that was to go to the boundary edge during a heat wave in Adelaide during a Test match. He vomited and then went back and bowled. "Yes, it was 104 in the shade for the whole match, and I bowled about 20 eight-ball overs I think, and of course you got dehydrated. I didn't just go to the boundary edge, I went into the dressing room actually, and I lay on the floor in the shower and was as sick as a dog, and I came out and bowled again. When I went out they said I was as white as a sheet, but still I went and bowled. I had to, there was no one else. It was so hot, Bill Edrich, he was trying to bowl the other end and he couldn't run up to bowl because of the heat, and then Doug Wright, he couldn't bowl either. It was pretty tough. That was the only time I left the field in any first-class match, although I think I did once here at the Oval leave the field because I had a touch of lumbago during a county game. That's the only other time I ever remember going off the field."

He obviously had a very strong physique, a powerful frame, but was it just the work he did that made him so strong and powerful, or did he do any special exercises? "I used to do a lot of training in the winter, running around the roads and that sort of thing, but I think I had a good, easy action. I didn't believe in running up any further than I had to. I don't think I strained, because the action was there and basically, obviously I was strong, but I think it was due to a lot of hard work over the growing period. You see the modern player today on television, people running round, and think that no one else ever did any training until five years ago or something, but of course we all did in the winter. But your actual everyday life was stronger and tougher. You were always lifting something, doing something, walking somewhere.

"When we were on the staff here before the war, we used to bowl all day in the nets. We used to get a season ticket from Woking to Waterloo, and then use it to go back to Vauxhall in order to save a penny on the tram, and then we'd walk from Vauxhall to the Oval and save another penny, and at night even though we were tired out we still walked back to Vauxhall. All that was good for you. We played at Nottingham, and we walked from the County Hotel, which was in the middle of Nottingham, down to the ground before play started, and then walk back at night. That was much better than doing the stretching that they do now."

He also had superb control over the ball. He had very big hands, which was obviously an advantage in that he could grip the ball, but where did he learn to bowl the way he did? "Practice, that's all. We were lucky that there were two of us. Eric and I loved practising, the same as I play golf, I love practising. I found it irritating in a way, when I was a tour manager, to hear so many players complaining that nets were boring. For me that's a sad thing, for a professional sportsman to say that it's boring to try to improve his skill, because that's what you're trying to do. I used to put a newspaper down and bowl at it from one stump. I'd bowl six balls and then Eric would bowl six balls. And we'd do it for hours on end. From the time I was 12 I think, after the war when we used to do it, I'd do it probably three times out of six. It was important to hit the newspaper and the stump because the newspaper was what I considered to be a good length, and as I say to so many of our bowlers today, the stumps are only 28 inches high and if you don't pitch it up enough, you won't hit the wicket. And you won't get anyone LBW, so that's two ways you're not getting anyone out. But you've got to pitch it up to do it, otherwise it bounces over the top. But you can't tell them, they won't listen."

He came on to the staff in 1938, and made his debut in 1939. Then there was the war, but as soon as he came back from the hostilities he made his England debut. "We came back here after the war, and Surrey's first match was at Lord's against MCC. And I got six wickets. Then after about four matches we had a Test trial. By then I'd half ruptured the top of my thigh muscle, but I used to tie it up and play, and I've still got a lump there now. I thought, 'I'm not going to cry off,' but I didn't tell anyone and our old trainer here, he used to pour hot water on it and everything else. I went to the trial and used to go into the toilet and tie it up so no one could see it, because I was afraid someone might say you can't play. I bowled 31 overs that day and I got Hammond and Hutton out, and then at the end of the trial they picked me for England. By the time the Test match came I'd got it better, but I just wonder what would have happened if I hadn't done that and said I wasn't fit. I might not have played for England, might not ever started a career. It just shows you, doesn't it?"

It must have been a surprise, albeit a very pleasant one, that he got in the England side as quickly as he did. "I didn't think about it really, I just thought I was lucky. I'm not a complicated person. I just got on with what I was going to do, and it didn't matter to me. It's difficult for people to understand that when you had seven years in the war, things are not quite so complicated. If you get through that, you think nothing else matters too much, so I just went and played, that's all. Obviously I was anxious to do well, but I can't think that I was ever really nervous. I was anxious of course, because I wanted to have a good start, but once I got out there I just bowled as I did normally, on a length, and they kept getting out. The ball moved a bit, and I got 11 wickets in that Test match."

And then in the second Test of that series he picked up another 11 wickets, seven in one innings, and four in the other. "That's right, I got 22 wickets in my first two Test matches. That was a good start, and that meant I was going to go to Australia, of course."

Alec Bedser had this big love affair with Australia. A lot of the big events in his career were centred on matches against Australia, but that first tour in 1946–47 must have been pretty tough. "It was hard. I was very green as a cricketer, although I'd got 130 wickets, but the pitches were perfect and it was no good an off-spin bowler or a slow left-hander trying to spin the ball. They never turned it an inch, even after five days the ball would never turn, and the only people that would turn the ball would be leg-spinners. That's why Australia had all leg-spinners, but your Jim Lakers and Tony Locks and anyone you could name wouldn't do it. Hedley Verity was always treated as a stock bowler out there, that's all he did because the ball didn't turn.

"It was really hard work, and you had some good players of course, a magnificent side. On our side they were mainly pre-war players, Len Hutton, Cyril Washbrook, Edrich, Compton, Joe Hardstaff, Dick Pollard, Bill Voce, John Langridge, Godfrey Evans came and Doug Wright, Peter Smith of Essex, Paul Gibb was the reserve wicket-keeper, and Norman Yardley. On the Australian side Barnes, Morris, Bradman, Hassett, Miller, Loxton, but Harvey wasn't in the side then. I remember we played at Melbourne in the second Test, and Bruce Doolan was number ten. When he played for Notts he got 170 wickets and

1,700 runs as well, so it just shows what a side they were. There was Lindwall and Miller of course, Bill Johnston who was a very fine bowler, underrated, McCool, Tallon was the wicket-keeper, they were a really fine side."

How much of a shock was it to find conditions as they were there? "The actual playing conditions weren't a shock. I just had to get on with it, but it was different. I knew what hot was like, because I'd been in North Africa, but there was no air conditioning. We travelled around Australia by train, and you got used to the heat. I loved every minute of it and I didn't want to come home. We left England on 31st August and we got home on 17th April. Eight months we were away."

And they were happy months, although not particularly successful months from the team's point of view. "Not for the team, but that didn't worry you, you just wanted to play. You tried hard. They were better than we were, and realised that we hadn't played for six years, and you couldn't expect anything else. The Australians had been playing Shield cricket."

After that tour, Bradman brought his famous side to England in 1948. Bedser had a degree of success against Bradman that other bowlers did not enjoy, and in fact on that '48 tour he went through a spell where he took the great man's wicket five consecutive times in Test matches. "I got him out a few times. I got him out six consecutive times actually. I got him out at Sydney in 1947, in the last innings of the Test match, when he had about 60. Then he came here and played against Surrey. He got a hundred, and I bowled him out then. We played at Nottingham and I got him out twice there. He got a hundred in one innings, nought in the other. And then twice at Lord's, so it was in fact six consecutive times, which I was proud of, of course."

So what was the secret? "I don't know. I swung the ball late and he was getting a bit older of course, he was 38, 39 and obviously wasn't as good as he was when he was younger. But he was still pretty good, he still averaged about 90 in the county season here. I think the crux of it was when I bowled them out in Adelaide, he came into bat and it was ten to six, and they all knew I bowled inswingers. I bowled about seven inswingers; by then I'd just begun to learn I could cut the ball, spin it, more by luck than otherwise at that stage. About the ninth ball, he thought it was going to swing away down the leg side, come across him, but when it pitched it went back the other way, and he must have missed it by six inches and it bowled him. So he then realised and in the second innings I did the same thing before he scored but it just missed the off stump, so he could have had a pair then, had the ball just not done as much. But I think what happened was that he realised that I could make the ball change course after it swung. So when he came to England

Bedser during practice at the Oval in 1950. He had been selected for England's winter tour to the West Indies

he had to play at more balls than he might have done otherwise, because he didn't know whether it was going to go the other way. Neither did I, so it didn't make any difference. But I spun it really, that's what I keep trying to emphasise, and they knew that it wasn't just pitching on the seam and down to luck; they realised I could do it."

It seems unlikely that he did not know whether the ball was going to move or not. "Well you don't know whether it's going to grip, that's the thing, so you've got to pitch it in the right spot, at least off stump or no nearer leg stump than that, because if it's going to go in, you don't want it to go down the leg side. Not on those surfaces. If it was a wet wicket I could say, yes, or if it was dusty, about four times out of six it would do it then, but on the pitches out there it would only grip now and again."

Alec Bedser was not the sort of bowler who would worry about a lack of support at the other end, and he had to carry the burden of the attack almost single-handed. Rather, he was the sort who would just get on and bowl because that is what he had to do. "I never thought about that. I didn't worry about a lack of support, all that jargon never came into it. When we played we just played. All this hunting in pairs nonsense you hear people say, I didn't mind because I was getting more wickets. If they weren't getting them at the other end I was getting them, so it suited me down to the ground. No, I never gave it a thought. I thought, I'm out here, I love doing it, I'm going to get on with it and do the best I can."

After he played against the Australians in England in 1948, he went on tour to South Africa in 1948/49, which would not have been much of a rest after playing Bradman's Australians. "I didn't mind, I loved it. I just wanted to go. We had a rest on the ship for two or three months, and that was enough I think. We went straight to South Africa in '48/49, then we had a rest, the next winter we didn't have anything."

While he professed to really enjoy touring, he did not take every opportunity to get abroad during the winters. "The first tour to the West Indies in 1947/48, Gubby Allen's tour, I'd bowled 3,000 overs in 18 months. In '46 I'd bowled 1,200 overs. I went to Australia and bowled 500 eight-ball overs, that's 700 six-ball overs, so that's 2,000 overs, and I came back and bowled another 1,200 overs here, so that was 3,200 overs in 18 months. By then I was tired out, and the Surrey president, Sir Henry 'Shrimp' Leveson Gower, said to Plum Warner, the chairman of selectors, that Surrey didn't want me to go, that I should have a rest, so I didn't go. We were never selected to go to India, which is a good way to correct what people often say to me. We only went on about one tour of India when I was playing Test cricket. In those days we had so many others, the Brian Stathams and the Tom Graveneys, they all went to India. Denis and Len and Cyril and Godfrey and myself, we weren't selected. It wasn't a question of declining to go, we just weren't selected, because they wanted to take the others, which they did, and they were fine cricketers anyway and it was an opportunity for them to play in a Test series."

If the tour to Australia in 1946/47 was hard, the tour there under Freddie Brown in 1950/51 must have been even harder. "I didn't find it hard, no, frankly I didn't. I was pretty fit and strong, I was getting people out, I didn't find it hard, no. It wasn't as hard as '46/47. We had a poor side, the worst-selected side I've ever seen I should think, with no disrespect to those who came, but they just weren't ready, they weren't good enough. It was a sad selection. If we'd selected the side with Jack Robertson, and Jack Ikin, and Edrich, and all sorts of bowlers, like Les Jackson of Derby, we'd have won the Ashes easily. I got

30 wickets at 16, and we bowled Australia out five times for under 200, and they only got 400 once, and yet we couldn't win the Ashes.

"If you look at our batting it was abysmal, and Denis only got 40 runs in four Test matches, and we lost two Test matches by 20-odd runs, so he only had to get 20 twice and we'd have won the Ashes! It was disappointing to me after I got 30 wickets at 16, the best performance by a pace bowler in Australia since Sydney Barnes, I should think. No one ever gives me much credit, they always talk about Larwood and Tyson, but my wickets were much cheaper than theirs, and I got more."

Frank Tyson featured prominently on the 1954/55 tour, when England did come back successful under Len Hutton, and that was not a happy tour for Bedser, who fell ill early on. "I got to Australia and I landed at Perth—I went by sea, you see—and I contracted shingles, and it was terrible. I was in bed for a fortnight and we got to New South Wales and by then I still had sores all over my back. I felt a bit stronger, and I'd been so used to weathering injuries, and saying, 'Right, I'll battle through this, I can do this.' So we played at Queensland, and it was one of those moist days up in the tropics there, and the ball moved around, and I got about three for 40 or something, and I thought, well I'm probably feeling all right, but it was all over very quickly. I didn't realise what effect shingles had on your constitution, so I played and I shouldn't have done.

"I should have gone home really, I had such a terrible back, I still had sores on my back, trying to bowl at 96 in the shade. I was a fool and I should have said no. If I hadn't played at Brisbane, I'd probably have been ready for Sydney, and I reckon I'd have got ten wickets at Sydney because the ball moved about all over the place, and I'd have got more at Melbourne, because it was the worst Test wicket I've ever seen in my life, when Tyson bowled them out. That was the wicket where the groundsman watered it over the weekend. I reckon 20 county bowlers would have got several wickets down there, all they had to do was pitch it on a length. But that's life, isn't it?"

While all this was going on, Surrey were carrying all before them in domestic cricket. The Championship was won seven consecutive times with a tremendous side to play county cricket. "From 1952 we had about eight of the blokes who all grew up together. We were all on the staff before the war, and were all mature cricketers by then. We were around 28, 29, and we could play, that's what it amounts to. It didn't matter who was put on to bowl, Stuart Surridge used to bowl a few in '52, and then there was myself, Peter Loader, Laker, Lock and Eric. All could bowl a length, all knew what they were doing, it didn't matter who you put on really.

"The one thing you did know was that they wouldn't give easy runs away, because they could bowl. We had a good side. Surridge was a great fellow to play with, because we grew up with him. We all played together when we were 16 and 17, so we all knew each other, and we'd call everyone everything, but it was forgotten in five minutes. We had wonderful spirit really, and we had some great catchers, we had Ken Barrington, Micky Stewart, Tony Lock and Stewie Surridge, and one season I think you'll find between them they caught 280-something catches. Of course, I always say the bowlers produce them. Without the bowlers producing the catches they wouldn't have been able to catch them, but nevertheless they were fine fielders.

"The pitches at the Oval took a bit of spin, the ball used to turn a bit, and they were quite slow, really. Now and again the weather would give you a green one of course, but in general terms the ball didn't come off, didn't zip. Because I could spin it and cut it, that's what helped me."

What he said about his colleagues reflects a positive, very professional outlook. "We were very positive, yes. We all thought we could play, and if we were bowling we were going to get them out, and it was imperative that we did win, because we wanted to keep winning the Championship. The more years we won, the more we wanted to win. We never thought of the word pressure, we just used to get out there and play. We got on well, we had a good lot of blokes. We still see each other now, still play golf together. We had a real good spirit here with the players. We'd all been through the war, most of us, and that made a difference."

Those seven Championship successes were an obvious highlight of his career, but among everything else that he achieved, the pinnacle must have been winning the Ashes back at the Oval in 1953. "It was, from my point of view. I think we came to the Oval and had to win the match, the other matches had been pretty tight. Talking about myself, I got 39 wickets at 17 in that series, and the next bloke I think was Johnny Wardle who got 12, and I felt that I contributed an enormous amount. Len went into three Test matches with only four bowlers, and no one else to bowl at all, so it was a good job I didn't break down!"

He was never likely to. "Well I didn't, but when I was on the selection committee picking sides, the first thing two or three of the chaps and the captain would say was, 'We must have X bowlers here, because someone might break down.' I don't know how Len would have gone on, but in three matches we only had four bowlers, and we bowled them out nevertheless. Actually I got 99 wickets in 15 consecutive Tests at 17 apiece, so when you work that out that's two series against Australia and one against South Africa. Not bad sides, and no one seems to record that anywhere. I suppose if I'd got one more, 100, it would have been, but that's over seven wickets a Test match!"

He took 14 at Trent Bridge in the 1953 series, followed by eight at Lord's, seven at Old Trafford and seven more at Headingley before his mere three at the Oval, all in the first innings. And at Lord's he became the first Englishman to get 200 wickets in Test matches. "There's a lot of 'I' about this! I don't really like talking too much about my own achievements, but seeing that the question has been asked, I'll answer it.

"At Nottingham I beat Syd Barnes' record, which was 189 Test wickets, and then at Lord's, Grimmett was the highest wicket-taker with 206 wickets, and I passed his, so I became the highest wicket-taker for a long time. But the thing that I've always been proud of was, when we only played Australia every other year, and only played five Test matches, I often pose the question, 'By the time I finished playing, who else had got 100 wickets for England against Australia, in their whole career?' People talk about Larwood and Tate, even Tyson some of them, but there were only four up to that time, and you had to go back to S.F. Barnes, Wilfred Rhodes, and Bobby Peel. I got 104 wickets against Australia in 20 Test matches, that's the thing I was most proud of, more than anything, because Australia were the best side.

"I loved playing against Australia and I loved going to Australia, and the people themselves are always wonderful to me, the Australians. They're so hospitable, and I've got so many friends there that it's been a great thing for me to be able to go back there a lot of times, and stay with these people and see them, because I get on well with the Australians."

Perhaps he sometimes felt disappointed, even bitter, that he was more appreciated as a cricketer in Australia than he was in England? "No, I'm not bitter and I'm not disappointed, but I am appreciated more in Australia, I think, than here. When people talk about cricketers, so many times you hear things mentioned, names written and mentioned about bowling feats. I think it's because I've never courted publicity much, and once I became a selector, which I did for 22 years, of course you couldn't write for the newspapers, or make any comment. So although I kept on the cricket scene by the fact I was doing that job, you didn't talk about yourself—well I wouldn't do that anyhow—but I think that may have been something to do with it, but anyway it's all gone, isn't it?"

He served over 20 years as a selector, which is a record in itself. A long, long time, so he must have enjoyed it to keep going that long. "Yes, I did enjoy being a selector, although in those days you didn't get anything, what it's cost me in earning capacity I don't know, but I enjoyed doing it. I like to be involved in the game. I wanted to try to do something if people felt I could. I don't want this old cliché about putting something back in it, but I felt I wanted to do it and enjoyed it a lot. I enjoyed being with the people who were running the game, and being on that footing, because you were part and parcel of it.

"You were involved in it all, and because of that I was asked to go with the Duke of Norfolk as his assistant manager, which was a great honour, and then I managed a couple of sides, which I enjoyed immensely, going to Australia. I was fortunate in that I was single to start with, and Eric was there all the time—we'd started our own business by then—and if I was away he could carry it on, so I could spare the time, and I've got to thank him for being there when I wasn't."

How different was it managing a tour to Australia as opposed to being there as a player? "It was much harder work managing a tour, particularly with the Duke of Norfolk—I had to do all the work then—but you had to worry much more about the detail. It's much easier being a player, you just get out and play and do your best, and then you've finished, haven't you? When you're managing the thing you've got to worry about everything. In the days of managers when I was with the Duke of Norfolk, there was far more work than they have to do now, because you got 50% of the gate to start with, you used to have to check all the takings every day, and check the turnstiles, and you had to do everything yourself, it was a lot of work to do. And all the accounts, you had to keep all the books because the Duke didn't, and there was always something to do. Nowadays there isn't any of that because it's just a guaranteed sum and that's it, so it was a lot of work but I enjoyed it. You didn't get much spare time, as you can imagine."

How did he get on with the Duke of Norfolk, as assistant manager to manager? "He was a marvellous man, a great fellow. Obviously I got to know him very well, because you would do if you lived with him for six months, and we became great friends. Obviously he didn't do much work except the front job, but he did many very kind things when we were there, he was such a nice man, what I would call a true gentleman. I used to get a car and drive him around, because he didn't know any of the Australian people. He didn't know his way around at all, so I got a car and used to take him to the races, which I enjoyed, and of course going with him you got the best treatment.

"I remember we were going to Flemington one day, to the Melbourne Cup. On the way I said, 'It's a funny thing, this is my fifth Melbourne Cup, and I only live ten miles from Ascot. I've never been to Ascot, and I've never seen the Derby.' He said,

'Would you like to go to Ascot?' and I said, 'I'd love to,' so he said, 'I'll send you some tickets.' That was November 1962, and in April Eric and I went down and stayed at Arundel with him, as we used to go down at weekends and stay with him. We were sitting having a cup of tea one day, and he said, 'By the way, do you still want to come to Ascot?' I said we'd love to, and he said, 'I'll send you the tickets.' So we go home and the tickets don't come, and we thought, 'He's too busy,' but a week before Ascot these tickets arrived, registered envelope. I've still got them at home now, mauve tickets they were. Queen's Car Park, Queen's Enclosure, the lot, and he sent us those tickets for seven years! That was just one little gesture; he was a great man."

Did he know his cricket as well? "Oh yes, he understood his cricket. He was a great stickler for punctuality and doing things right. If someone misbehaved, that was the end of it as far as he was concerned. I used to pick him up at his hotel and he was never late, and I used to say, 'What time do you want to go to the ground?' He might say, 'Ten o'clock,' and I'd say, 'Well, the traffic's bad, I can't park too long outside here. I'll get the car and I'll be outside here at ten o'clock.' He said, 'Well, let's synchronise our watches,' and I'd drive up dead on ten, and he'd be walking down the steps dead on ten. That's the sort of chap he was."

As chairman of selectors it was inevitable that Bedser was open to a lot of criticism. It was likely that anyone in that position would take a lot of flak from the public, because in the public's mind there's never been a good selector. But he thought he was doing a good job, and the results showed that he was doing a good job. "I think we did reasonably well when I was chairman, we won a lot of matches. You never do things that everyone agrees with. I felt that you did the best you could with what was available, and I used to keep saying to people that selectors don't make players; it's the system that makes the players. The counties have got to produce the cricketers, and they should be able to come to a Test match and play. If they don't play to the best of their ability, then they've let you down.

"All right, they're human, but when you read about how you should blood people in Test matches and bring them along, I couldn't understand all that. I thought, you're either good enough to play or you're not, and you've got to have something about you, you've got to be that little bit different to be any good. I then tried to look at myself and thought, well, perhaps I was a bit lucky because I came back at the end of the war. After six years in that, this so-called word pressure never came into your being, you never thought about that. You wanted to do well, but if you failed you knew very well you'd come back to your county again. If I'd played a Test match and I thought I hadn't bowled too well, and perhaps only got two or three wickets, I used to come back here to the Oval and say to myself, 'If I don't get five wickets in this match, they won't pick me for the next Test.' That's how we used to think.

"Now it doesn't matter what you do in county cricket, does it? They still play in the Test matches. I don't think that's very good for the other fellows. I never thought anyone had a right to play for England. I don't agree with the squad system, because it must create the feeling among the other players on the county scene that they can't get in. I hear it said, 'You've upset his confidence,' and this sort of thing, but if you're good enough and you fail, you expect not to play, I should think. But I've always tried to understand how blokes felt, because I knew what it felt like to be dropped myself. I always tried to tell them so they knew, but I never felt it was my duty just to keep them there, because they felt that they ought to be given a chance, as they call it.

"We made mistakes when you pick players, but you always tried to pick the ones that fitted in with what you were trying to do, and also those who you felt potentially had the ability to do it. They may let you down, they may not play up to their potential and things may go wrong, the wicket may go wrong. But once the game started, once you've tossed the coin, I then used to say to the captain, 'Now it's your job,' and I'd never poke my nose in. I always used to say, 'If you want any help, if you feel you want to ask, by all means,' but I would never go to him and say, 'Now I want you to do this,' because once you did that, you were then in a cleft stick, because if he failed he could just turn round and say, 'The chairman told me to do this.' I would never do that. I would say, 'Right, it's your job now, you must get on with it, you helped to pick the team.' Which they did. If there was something that I felt was radically wrong discipline-wise, that's a different thing, but conducting the game, I would never force my opinion on the captain as to what he should do, that was his job."

In 1987 he was made president of Surrey. Did that mean much to him? "That was wonderful, and Eric's president this year [1990], so that's two of us. It's difficult for younger people to understand. When we walked through those Hobbs Gates in the first place we weren't allowed in the pavilion even, and as for coming into the committee room, you just weren't there, you were in another world. I remember when we used to play out here, we used to look up at this balcony and think, 'Why can't I get up there?' seeing the committee standing up here, watching you play, and it's all happened, so it's a great honour."

He was inseparable from his twin brother Eric all the way through his career, except for the fact that Eric did not make it to the very highest standard as a player, only by virtue of the fact that he failed to get into the England side. Was that a disappoint-

ment for him? Did he feel that his career would have been complete if Eric could have come right the way along the road with him? "I'd have liked him to, and he would have done if he'd left Surrey, which he could have done. He'd have got 1,000 runs and 100 wickets every year if he hadn't been here. Because he only used to bowl when Jim Laker didn't want to bowl, most of the time. He bowled on all the good wickets, and he still got 80 to 90 wickets at about 23.

"If he was playing today he'd walk into the England side. I don't say that as a brother, you've only got to look at his record. In '49 he got 1,800 runs at 36, and 80 wickets at about 21, only bowling on good wickets, he didn't bowl on any turners because Jim and Locky bowled on them. It's disappointing, but we didn't want to split up, we wanted to stay at the Oval here together, but if he'd gone to any county, they'd have had him. Of course you had to have a two-year qualification in those days, which made it more difficult to move, but if he'd gone, even then he'd have walked into the England side, because he could bat."

Eric went on playing for one more season after Alec retired, finally giving up in 1961. He did not follow Alec into administration and it was for that service that Alec was knighted. Eric, the marginally older brother, died in 2006, but Alec soldiered on until 2010, when English cricket lost one of its greatest yeoman standard bearers.

Colin Ingleby-Mackenzie
1933–2006

Colin
Ingleby-Mackenzie

*I*T COULD BE ARGUED *long into the night, and often is, whether a captain is as good as his team or the team is as good as the captain. Even those who swear by the former code have to admit, however grudgingly, that the skipper does have an influence on the performance of the players around him, in some cases quite disproportionate to his personal ability. It should not be suggested that Hampshire's captain when the county's first Championship title was secured in 1961 was anything other than a thoroughly good player who contributed more than his fair share of runs to that success. It is just that the team was very much a reflection of their captain's character; it was* his *team.*

The captain in question was Alexander Colin David Ingleby-Mackenzie, born at Dartmouth in Devon in 1933. He arrived at Hampshire via Eton and made his debut for the county in 1951. By the time of his retirement in 1965 he had played in 343 first-class matches, scoring 12,421 runs at an average of 24.35. He hit 11 centuries, recorded 1,000 runs in a season five times, and held 205 catches as well as making one stumping. What those statistics do not reflect is the way he played his cricket. He attacked. That meant that his batting average was lower than it might have been, because he was not one to massage the figures behind the barricades of not outs. It is for that, as much as the 1961 Championship success, three years after he took over the captaincy and four years before he gave it up, that he will forever be remembered by Hampshire folk.

Those followers of Hampshire cricket will subscribe to the theory that the team he led was a reflection of the captain's personality, but to what extent did the captain himself accept that view of his players? "I think the thing about them was that they were all able to accept a very young captain, which I find a most unusual character study of them. The essence of and the core of one's success, which I am very proud of because they were a fantastic team to play with and work with, really was a man called Desmond Eagar who I took over from in 1958.

"We were joint captains in 1957, which was a recipe for a pretty good disaster because he had his style and I had mine. Basically it didn't really work, although we had lots of fun but he was not really a cocktailer, which I must confess at moments I was. He led in a different sort of a way. He was a strong disciplinarian, although I certainly did have certain codes and ways that I thought we could build up strategies and try and win our matches. I think both of us wanted to win, and that was the key question. We were different people, and he was wonderful in leading me through to be able to take over the captaincy of seasoned professionals and campaigners at a fairly young age."

At what point did cricket become part of life of the young Ingleby-Mackenzie? "I started my keenness down at Dartmouth College in Devon. There was a lovely old professional called Hanniman down there, a wonderful guy. I used to play and I couldn't think of anything else and in those days it was just cricket. There was no wine or women involved in my life, I just thought, smelt and dreamt cricket and I thought he was a wonderful man.

"My father was very keen on playing cricket and realised, as Hercule Poirot might put it, that the little grey cells were not quite as plentiful as one might have hoped. He could see, I think, that cricket was clearly going to be my first love. How good I was going to be I don't really know, but I went to Ludgrove Preparatory School aged eight to 13. The headmaster was a man called Alan Barber, who had been captain of Yorkshire, and he was much keener on me playing cricket than passing my academic examinations to go to Eton. I then went to Eton and my housemaster was completely and totally dedicated to sport. Although he was keen on the Greek, Latin, History and all the other arts, he was really a great sports enthusiast. He sort of encouraged me through Eton days and led into my naval days, and then wonderfully happy days with Hampshire."

Eton must have been exactly the right environment in which to learn to play cricket because the pitches were invariably good. "Agar's Plough or Upper Sixpenny are strange names to quite a lot of people who haven't played there, but generally speaking I think that the wickets there were superb and encouraged the amateur of the day. Certainly people like Denis Compton and Keith Miller, who used to come to play there, would have agreed. Mind you, they used to get out pretty quickly to go to Windsor races.

"When I was playing in the '50s and '60s there were very many more amateurs, like Peter May and Colin Cowdrey, from public schools who played first-class cricket and who were educated on really magnificent wickets. You learned how to play forward, you knew how to go back, the bounce was even and so you did your apprenticeship on superb wickets. I was coached by a top professional coach, Jack O'Connor, who played for Essex and England. He was a wonderful coach and I had all possible advantages. Maybe when you watched me play you'd realise that some of those advantages were thrown away, but it gave one a hell of a start and I was very lucky."

As he mentioned, he went into the Navy when he left Eton, but what did that do for his cricket? "I was lucky again in as much [as] I was generally posted during the summer to nice places like Portsmouth or Dorset, where I started in HMS *Indefatigable*, which was a huge great aircraft carrier and as an ordinary seaman it was tough going. Life in a hammock wasn't the ideal preparation if you had to bat all day or field all day. It was a rich experience and actually there were some very good matches. F.S. Trueman, for instance, was playing for the Combined Services and the RAF, and I was lucky enough to be selected for the Navy in both 1952 and 1953 when I had just left school, and they were exciting times.

"They were good stepping stones. There were moments when one might have felt it would be fun to go to university and play for Oxford, or try to play for Oxford, and I was going to go up. But then I decided, if I was going to do my national service, which I had to do, and then perhaps go to work, which my father was keen on, in a factory up in Yorkshire, then I should not go up to Oxford as it would be too long before I would start earning a needy crust. I had two marvellous years in the Navy and the cricket was very good. There were lots of professionals in those days doing their national service, and it was very competitive. Army versus the Navy were tough battles."

Ingleby-Mackenzie did not give the immediate impression of being an "ordinary seaman" as he put it, so how long was it before he began to move up a deck or two? "I was very lucky because my father just happened by chance to be an admiral, and so when navigation exams or communications exams came up, I have a feeling that the decimal point may have been moved slightly to the right. So I sneaked through and became a midshipman, which made life very much easier for me and it was great fun and a great experience. It was two years I wouldn't have missed."

It might have been a coincidence that he finished up playing for Hampshire, or that his time in the Navy gave him an affiliation with the county, or was there another connection? "The connection was that when I was in my last year at my preparatory school, Ludgrove, my father was then at Haslar Hospital down in Gosport. I went to have some nets and coaching at Easter from a lovely old fellow called Jim Bailey, who bowled left-hand for Hampshire over many, many years. He was a great character and one afternoon, end of March or April I think it was, he kept on bowling half-volleys because I think Desmond Eagar was on the horizon somewhere and the president, who was also a great friend of my father called Harry Altham, president of MCC in later years, came and watched. Jim Bailey, instead of bowling me the one that pitched on the off then knocks the leg out, or vice versa, just bowled me half-volleys and said, 'Well done, my boy.' And Harry Altham came over and said, 'What's his name?' and 'How does he play?' and 'He's not the worst left-hander I've ever seen.' They said if ever I was interested in perhaps playing cricket later on, that they would be very interested.

"At that time I was totally ecstatic at the thought of playing county cricket. My head was in the moon and in the stars. I thought this was something else and so, being a fairly loyal guy at heart, if there was any conceivable thought of playing county cricket, the only other place I suppose I could have gone was through residential qualifications in London, so it would have been Middlesex. But somehow Hampshire had built up some interest, they dangled the carrot and it was too exciting for someone who had never even considered it not to have them at the top of my list."

Not everyone of that age watched cricket as opposed to playing at every opportunity, but Ingleby-Mackenzie was different. "I watched a lot and I had lots of heroes. Walter Hammond, Denis

Compton, Bill Edrich. One's formative years, I would suppose, were when I was at Eton or preparatory school, and having been there from 1941 to '46, and then from '46 to 1951, there were a lot of wonderful years. It was the Compton-Edrich era for Middlesex, and Jack Robertson. I watched a lot of cricket at Lord's, living in London which I did, but the love of cricket has always been embedded in me and obviously county cricket was something I would always be very excited by."

He made his debut for Hampshire in 1951, against Sussex at Bournemouth, without covering himself in glory. He was out for nought, but how clearly did he remember the match? "I was very, very nervous and it rained, I believe, for a lot of the match. I was bowled by Alan Oakman, who was a lifelong friend of mine, and he came up afterwards and said, 'Ingles, I gave you a full toss, and I've never seen an Etonian not hit a full toss for four. Your performance was pathetic so I then bowled you out. I'm sorry.' I've always been friends with him, but he thought it was just one more wicket given to him on a plate, and he was right.

"The thing I remember most about the match was that it was rain-affected, and I got very friendly with a guy called Phil Mead, whom I think most people in Hampshire will remember. He and I had something in common, although I think that our batting prowess didn't run parallel because he was also a left-hander, but he was a wonderful player. But he was mad keen on racing and so I sat and talked to him for hours in the pavilion about racing. He also talked to me about cricket and he was a very instructive and very interesting person. I became friends with him and I think that Hampshire cricket was what his life was made for. What a lovely guy."

Who was playing in the Hampshire side when he made his debut? "Desmond Eagar was the key man, having taken over the captaincy after the war, and there was Neil McCorkell, Neville Rogers played a very major part when I first started playing, and somebody who I think was closest to my heart, Leo Harrison. He was the wicket-keeper and was a wonderful guy; a unique personality, a marvellous wicket-keeper, he could also field brilliantly. He was a very useful batsman and he was able to tickle up my social interests as well, because he fitted nicely into his dinner jacket in the evening when we used to go off together. He liked racing and was keen on gambling in the right sort of financial areas, and he was a great companion. They were always a marvellous side to watch in my opinion, but they'd never done very well in the County Championship, so it was something that just interested me as to whether we might ever be able to sneak them up the table a little bit."

As indicated by the reference to Leo Harrison, Hampshire at the time were noted as a very sociable side. Add to that the fact that they were a very lively, good side to watch, and perhaps there is a clue to why they failed to win the Championship earlier than they did. "I don't think so. I think there's too much said about the dangers of the social life in the media nowadays. I think it is important you understand that you're away an enormous amount of time. There are 11, 12, 13 of you, a lot of them are married, you're playing cricket day after day. If you're working in the City you finish at six o'clock perhaps, and you probably start fairly early, but there you go home in the evening. In county cricket you go away to Northants, to Derby, to Worcester, to Lancashire or to Yorkshire and you're away for a long time. I think it's important that you can relax and I think that it's exaggerated what goes on. I think if an attractive young lady crosses your path, in my view you are the luckier for her being there, but she doesn't influence your performance the next day. You have a few drinks because you take pounds off during the day as you've been running around like a dervish. You build up team spirit by being together and I actually think in moderation it's a very, very good catalyst for success."

There is a celebrated quotation attributed to Ingleby-Mackenzie in which he laid down the rules for socialising during matches. Was it true that he said everyone should be on the ground by the start of play? "Well, not quite. That was slightly exaggerated. I must admit that I think the bright life should be encouraged. You can get very boring, day in day out, by asking everybody to be in bed by breakfast, as I used to say, which is a different approach. But I think if you're always in bed pm rather than am, I think you're a duller guy for it and I think we all had a lot of fun.

"Some were used to going to bed early, like Derek Shackleton, who looked after his training and who was a very sensible guy, but if you looked at the Hampshire team when I was playing it was about 50-50. Some of us would be giving it a bit of a *craic* but that was our lifestyle and we played better for it. We were more relaxed and our reactions were better. Others wanted to go to bed early, and wanted to concentrate, and needed that extra sleep."

Ingleby-Mackenzie was legendary for his love of horse racing, but where did that interest stem from? "I don't know. I think it probably started when I was at school at Eton. I think that everybody has different boxes in their system, so you're either an artist or you're a musician or you're a fantastic hockey player or something. I suppose somewhere I had a little racing box in me that somehow gets switched on and I then became more and more interested. At school you meet friends who are keen racing people, and when I was at school the great racing trainer Peter Cazalet's son, Edward, was there, Charles Benson was in the same house as me at school, and he became the Scout in the Daily Express. He was a great character and encouraged one's interest and somehow it steered me towards a very happy and exciting life. I think it's something you can follow very easily when playing cricket, because when you're waiting to go in to bat you have hours of time, and it is quite a good distraction just to follow something that doesn't take up all your concentration. You're taking an interest in something without taking your mind off what you're meant to be doing in five, ten minutes or half an hour by going out and trying to bat."

He had this great cavalier image and stories abound about him getting out to hear the result of a race, or asking for new gloves being brought out to the middle along with the result of the 3.30 from Newbury or wherever. Was there any truth in that or were they just apocryphal? "They're all absolutely true, of course they are. I mean I conducted myself on the field to the maximum of self-control and discipline but I must confess that my mind did wander on occasions. I think it's important that I kept an interest in what was going on outside, because in a long day in the field you need a little bit of distraction. Otherwise you get so bogged down and you get locked in into what is going on and I liked a little bit of outside music. I think that the team rather enjoyed the idea that one did have an interest in the horses. I tried to lead them on the sticky path to disaster, but most of them were pretty sensible, but I think that I did encourage some of them to realise that racing was fun, and actually to place a wager was quite exciting.

"I tried to get Derek Shackleton, in his benefit match when there wasn't a great crowd down at Bournemouth, to put some of the take on a horse called 'Time and Again', and it won at 100 to 8, but I'm afraid even I couldn't persuade Old Shack to part with money to put on this horse. He regretted it afterwards, but laughed about it."

Famous for his approach to the game, and to life in general, did being something of a gambler help him with captaincy? "I don't say you want to be a gambler but I think you want to be able to relate the odds of what you are doing. I think captains need to have an element of the gambling instinct, and we certainly did when we won the Championship. I think we won 19 matches out of 32, and an enormous number of them were on declarations. Now it certainly wasn't all my brilliant moments of declaration, because I had lots of help from the dressing room with flags thrown out of the window and that sort of thing, but during those matches you certainly had to be able to equate the odds. That makes for somebody who perhaps is more accustomed to the gambling element in the nervous system and who knows what the odds are, particularly during the last hour or half-hour of the match."

Such a philosophy does not strike so much of cavalier gambler, but more of someone very cold and calculating. "It was cold and calculating, but we wanted to win, and I dangled the carrot to the media and the press about wine, women and song, be in bed by three o'clock tomorrow afternoon or whatever it was, but generally speaking we were out to win, and as keen to win as anybody else. Equally, you have to feed a line to the press which keeps them involved in what you're doing, and that's all we were really trying to do. I'm certainly not a cold, calculating guy but the end product is that we wanted to win, therefore we took the odd chance and threw the balls in the air, hoping they came down on our side of the wrapper."

Despite feeding the press with lines supporting the image of the carefree cavalier, opposing captains claimed that he did not actually give very much away. "No, I was as mean as hell. I was brought up on Vic Cannings and Derek Shackleton, who were pretty tough cookies, and I bowled Derek Shackleton a lot. He was able to bowl a lot because he was fit and he was a fantastic machine. He could be just as effective on a medium-pace or slow wicket or even on a turning wicket, as he was on a fast seamer at Portsmouth or at Lord's. He was unique and he played it pretty tight, as did Peter Sainsbury.

"Then there was Butch White, and you can't pretend that he was anything else but a wild gambler. He came careering in and bowled very, very fast and you never knew from one second to the next what was going to happen, but that was exciting stuff. Henry Horton batted in a very tough, ruthless way. You've got to have, in any side, a core of people who can give you a platform from which to launch, and they were certainly the key performers."

The mix was absolutely right, and it was a side that he was taking over from Desmond Eagar, who was very influential in his career. "He was a great guy, a great enthusiast and a wonderful captain, and he was as good a fielder as I was bad. I just haven't got enough superlatives to justify his existence in Hampshire cricket, and the dedication which he gave to the game and to me. He was absolutely superb and it was due to him that my presence was made so easy. There wasn't half the side saying, 'Who is this horrible little Etonian at 24 coming in to captain the side?' which could easily have happened, and it would have been impossible with those old seasoned campaigners.

"Desmond ensured that this was not the case, and also set me up with a wonderful side, which made a tremendous difference, because there wasn't only Derek Shackleton's bowling, but also there was Roy Marshall, and he and Jimmy Gray were a terrific opening partnership. I came straight into Marshall and Gray and what better scene could there be, with Horton as the absolute rock at the core of the innings? That was a marvellous start, and then you had Butch White and Malcolm Heath and Derek Shackleton obviously, and Peter Sainsbury, Leo Harrison

*Ingleby-Mackenzie leads Hampshire onto the field in their
Championship-winning season, 1961*

keeping wicket, Danny Livingstone batting, Mike Barnard, Alan
Wassell—they were all great players. It made for a really lovely
atmosphere and, to be honest, a very easy job.

"The time was right in 1958 when I started, which was the year
when I thought we couldn't possibly do well. Little did I realise
when we cruised into August that we should have won the
Championship. Then that slipped away, we got a bit nervous, we
didn't have enough drinks to calm our nerves and we came second
to Surrey. I suppose it was disappointing but it gave one the sort
of feel of what might be possible, but we just couldn't make it.
Then in 1961, not too long to wait, we achieved what we had
never done before, which was beyond one's wildest dreams."

*He remarked that when he assumed the captaincy there was not
any resentment to this fancy chap from Eton taking over the
hardened professionals. The time was right, but it might well not
have happened in some counties other than Hampshire.* "They
had a reputation. Lionel Lord Tennyson was a sort of wild
lunatic who was a wonderful captain, with tremendous

character and charisma who did his own thing. He was a tremendous player, captaining England, and he was a very forceful personality.

"I think that some of the southern counties, like Hampshire, Kent and Surrey more easily accept that these young reprobates come in and take over the captaincy. It's more accepted by the seasoned pros. They're marvellous to accept the situation but on the other hand, I sometimes question whether they in fact want the job. I remember talking to Fred Titmus, who became captain of Middlesex for a time, and he thought it was a very easy job. It's not an easy job, and he very soon realised it was a very difficult job actually being captain of a county side.

"I think a lot of professionals think that they've got it all, they've got the experience and they know the cricket game, as they certainly do, but it isn't just an on the field activity being captain. 25 hours a day you got 11, 12, 13, probably 16 players who you're permutating around to make your team over a whole season. You've got their domestic problems, you've got their lifestyle and it's a management system. It isn't that easy; it's not difficult but it isn't as easy as a lot of people think. They believe that you go out, shout heads or tails, win the toss or lose it, and away you go boys; let's win the match and on to the next one. There's a little bit more to it, and there are more subtleties than meet the eye.

"I think you've got to naturally enjoy what you're doing. I was lucky that the players accepted my natural desire to have a good time, and incorporated into that was that I wanted them to have a good time. I fully realise that by winning I was helping them make more money. A little money in the pocket helps one's attitude to life, and I naturally enjoyed what I was doing, but I was very lucky to have the players that I did to make my job easier."

If you look at team photographs of most Championship-winning sides, you see six on the back row, and five in front with the captain in the middle. A photograph of Hampshire in 1961 featured four at the front—Jimmy Gray, Ingleby-Mackenzie himself, Roy Marshall and Derek Shackleton—and, with the 12th man, eight others ranged along the back. The four in the front were really the core of the team. "I don't think anybody was the core, to be honest. Those were certainly four key players. As for Roy Marshall, the words, the books, the figures speak for themselves. He was a fantastic operator and in 1961, which was his benefit year, he was an even greater operator. We were winning, he had his West Indian approach of playing strokes all around the wicket, and he had a very good tactical cricket brain. He was enormously helpful to me in giving me advice about change of bowling, or opposition batting weaknesses, and what to do on winning the toss and in selecting sides. We had a very small committee to give help and advice, comprising of him, Jimmy Gray, Leo Harrison, Derek Shackleton and Peter Sainsbury, although it only came through him, but we worked as a team. We probably didn't have enough seats or something, but I think it was very much a team effort with obviously those four of the highest calibre.

"The interesting thing about Shackleton was that he was the key, along with Butch White. Derek could move the ball both ways, and as the senior campaigner was obviously someone who had to be respected as to which end he wanted. It was equally obvious that Butch White, lovely guy, lunatic, good left-handed golfer and tremendous supper up in the evenings, was probably one of the quickest bowlers in county cricket at the time, and he had to bowl with the wind because otherwise the true value of his speed would not be rewarded. So, as a broker, that was the only element of subtlety I occasionally had to use. When there was a slight slope and somebody had to bowl into the wind up a hill and it was downhill with the wind, it was very clear which job should be given to which bowler, but equally clear that Derek Shackleton, as the senior bowler, might easily have been very difficult, and he never once was. He was superb and therefore he made my job very, very easy. I was a very lucky guy.

"With Butch White one knew where one wants to set a field, but it was a question of where he was going to bowl and it was a very hairy situation at times. But he was a lovely guy to have, because he was a great destroyer. He was the only bowler we had who was very likely to get out one of the first three batsmen in the opposition. He could equally easily destroy the tail through sheer speed and terror, because not only were the batsmen frightened, but I think Butch was equally frightened because he did not know where the ball was going to go. He would get rid of a tail, which is often a very difficult thing to do, particularly in a declaration innings where the declaration had gone wrong. With the other side trying to block to save the match, he would then bowl out eight, nine, ten and jack. He was a match-winner, which was what we wanted.

"Also, he won occasional matches by his batting. I can remember one match in 1961 against Gloucestershire at Portsmouth, which helped us on our road to thinking that we might win the Championship, because he slogged 30-odd right against the odds. We had no chance of winning the match, but through sheer power and lots of luck he won us a match which we never thought for one second, with ten minutes to go, we had any chance of winning."

Having finished second in the Championship before, but never having won it, there must have been a few jitters around the place as the title run-in was on. "There certainly were. When you're coming up against Middlesex and Yorkshire and Surrey, who were seasoned campaigners who had always been in the thick of it, and then there was Hampshire. I was ringing up my bookmaker and we were still 20 to 1, and I told him that we were going to win it. He said we had no chance with star England players in all the other counties, so even right up to the line I couldn't really pretend that we were going to win, until I suppose midway through the afternoon when we did actually win it, against Derbyshire in Bournemouth.

"It was quite an amusing situation because Harold Rhodes was batting, and he was the son of Dusty Rhodes, who was umpiring. We were getting fairly desperate at this stage, and they were going to play it out because they didn't appear likely to get runs. I kept on going to Father Rhodes and suggesting that he might kindly tell his son that this is no good. He could get no honour and glory for saving this match, but think if he goes down as the player who was actually in the match when Hampshire won the Championship. Dusty told me not to worry and that Harold would not still be there at the end, but it all worked out satisfactorily in the end without father's intervention, but we were lucky.

"I think there was a tremendous feeling for us. I've got to say that in a lot of declarations we got, and a lot of the way the other side batted right down to have a go in our declaration matches, there was a sympathetic streak for us. They would go on a little further, because they wouldn't mind getting beaten by Hampshire because there had been such a long tradition of success from the major counties. I think they went down the extra couple of batsmen in other words, when six wickets were down they would normally have said, 'That's enough, we'll go for a draw,' but with us they probably went down to eight wickets, when we could then fire in the main bowlers, who suddenly got the wicket that made the big difference. They just went that little bit further to give us the edge all the time, which was a great advantage."

Mentioning that there was still another match to go, against Yorkshire after the title had been secured, brought a characteristic response from Ingleby-Mackenzie. "I believe Yorkshire came down and played, but I can't remember much about it. I do remember going out on the field, and one or two people saying a few things pointing me towards the middle, and I think I managed to throw the coin in the air. I do remember Roy Marshall making a brilliant hundred, but we were beaten by Yorkshire and they were adamant they would have taken the title if we hadn't beaten Derbyshire, because that would have swung the Championship the other way. But we had a pretty good celebration, and although earlier I said I didn't think it made a major difference, I think if you've run the whole of Bournemouth dry of champagne, gin, vodka, whisky and any other drink you care to mention, you're perhaps not quite as sharp as the Yorkshire side were in those three days."

Ingleby-Mackenzie alluded to the fact that there was a certain warmth of feeling towards Hampshire in 1961. Everyone, apart from those who had been denied the Championship, seemed pleased that Hampshire had won it because of the way they played their cricket. "I think they liked to play us very much. I was lucky that they were a very nice side to play against and we didn't have any difficult players. I think we were a popular side, and I don't know whether I should say this but I think certainly all the team I played with were popular with the other sides. The stars, Roy Marshall and Derek Shackleton, were very popular and people loved watching them. We were good losers, and I hope good winners, and that is something I've always been proud of. It wasn't really my doing but I certainly hope I was involved in making Hampshire a nice side to play against."

Ingleby-Mackenzie in full flow, 1961

It must have been difficult in subsequent seasons, because by then it had been seen that Hampshire could win, and other counties would not have given them too many favours in terms of declarations, whereas they might have done earlier. "It was more difficult, because when I take you out to dinner tonight and give you caviar and Bollinger, you'll be very pleased with me, but then tomorrow night it's scrambled egg and bacon, and you might still be quite pleased to see me but it probably hasn't quite got the glitter. I admit that we'd achieved something we didn't really think we could quite achieve, and it was very difficult to keep the edge going. One of my problems was that I went out to Australia after we won the championship and got hepatitis, which is a pretty ugly disease, and I didn't really feel that well at the beginning of the 1962 season. I lost a bit of edge and although the other years were tremendous fun and I enjoyed playing, the challenge from 1958 to 1965 was quite a long time. It's like if you have a life's ambition to win the Derby, and you do, however spectacular other races might be, it's not quite the same.

"I still loved playing county cricket, and meeting all the people one met going to all the different grounds, which is an excitement in itself. We'd play anywhere and we went to the Isle of Wight or the Channel Islands, we went to Germany and various other places, which I think endorses what I've already said that we had a fantastic collection of players with a wonderful team spirit. Right the way through, wherever we went, there was a fun aura about what we were doing and what we were trying to do. Socially and with all that playing ability, it all combined to give us a most happy welcome wherever we went."

Perhaps any feeling of anti-climax after 1961 was increased by the fact that there was only the County Championship to be won at that time in domestic cricket. "Yes. We then started getting into the Gillette Cup and all these new one-day tournaments which I didn't play in. I did play in the Gillette Cup and we got to the semi-final, but I never really got very involved in that. I would have thought with the side that won in 1961 we would have had a tremendous chance of winning a few of these one-day tournaments. We had lots of attacking batsmen, good defensive bowlers and a very good fielding side, which are really the three criteria for success in one-day cricket."

Whenever a side wins a Championship, the spotlight goes on the captain. In many cases the question is then asked as to whether he has the potential to transfer his qualities to the Test arena.

Did Ingleby-Mackenzie ever feel that he was close to Test cricket? "It would have been a tremendous challenge, and I can't pretend that if you had rung me up as chairman of selectors and said I was doing it, [then] I would have put the telephone down and been very excited.

"I suppose the only chance I ever had was the 1962 tour of Australia. We'd just won the Championship and my batting average, or cricket average shall we say, was at that time the highest it could have been. That was really, I suppose, the only possible moment I could ever have thought of it. But E.R. Dexter got the captaincy, and he was such a fantastic player and a marvellous cricketer that one couldn't ever begrudge it. I think there was a sense of the expected. It was like a horse race. I was certainly the outsider of two, but if I'd been the outsider of three I might have fancied my chances, because they very often win.

"I can't pretend that it was anything other than very exciting, because I would have loved the chance of having the best spinner, the best left-arm bowler, the two best opening bowlers, two best opening batsmen and wicket-keeper. I would have thought one's job is easier than perhaps captaining a county. So purely out of interest and excitement and honour, it would have been something that I would have very much treasured. I don't think I was the right guy, although it would have been exciting to have been given the opportunity, particularly in Australia. It would have been a major excitement for me. But I think that Ted was the right guy, but I cannot pretend it wouldn't have been exciting to have won the day."

He might not have gone on an official tour, but he certainly saw the world playing cricket because he went on a lot of unofficial tours. "I became a sort of professional unofficial tourist. My great advantage was that I was able to keep wicket. When I was captain in 1961 I kept wicket quite a lot for Hampshire, because Leo Harrison broke a finger when we were playing Glamorgan in Swansea. On all these tours they look for a sort of dogsbody number two wicket-keeper and so I went on an enormous number. Cavaliers tours, Jim Swanton was very kind to invite me to captain a number of tours, the Duke of Norfolk's tour to the West Indies. In fact I've been very lucky in that I hardly had a winter when I didn't go on some sort of overseas tour. All played to a very high level, for they were tremendous sides.

"I remember when we went to South Africa with the Cavaliers side organised by Ron Roberts. We were a terrific side, with people like Tyson, Graveney, Ian Craig, Bert Sutcliffe, Denis Compton, Gary Sobers, Richie Benaud—a really unbelievable side. I was very lucky and played with all sorts of cricketers of every nationality, every colour, from Abbas Ali Baig, the Nawab of Pataudi, Bishen Bedi, Indians, South Africans, West Indians, Englishman, Australians. All of them, no matter what county, country, nationality or colour, were wonderful to play with and against."

All those tours, the County Championship title, mention of the England captaincy must have made it a difficult decision to give up playing cricket. "I'd done eight years and although it doesn't sound a lot, we'd reached a sort of peak in the middle. It seems young to have retired as a captain at 32, but when I retired in 1965, eight consecutive years was quite a long time. Funnily enough I would have almost quite enjoyed just trying to appear as a player, to see whether I was good enough. I might have had to play a little bit better. As a captain you have so many things to think about, and I tended to drift further down the order from five to six. I was trying to bring on young players and educate them, and also I was probably not as good, which is a rather important reason.

"I think after eight years one had had a fairly good crack, and the other thing probably more important is that one had to look at one's future. Also, I had to get down to a bit of hard work. I somehow felt, and I owed it to my parents, and everybody else who gave me such a good start, that really one had to look to finding a job in which one could still be involved with cricket but not actually playing.

"Administration didn't appeal to me. I had worked for Slazenger's and my insurance broking team while I was playing cricket, so I had a knowledge of that. As for actual cricket administration, no offer came and presented itself on a plate. I was involved in both these areas, and it really seemed the obvious route to take. I suppose you could think of various administrative jobs, but I don't know how well they paid. That wasn't really a serious point, but I think that didn't really cross my path. I was involved in the other areas, so I had a sort of lead into them, and it seemed to me to be logical to continue in either the sporting field or the insurance field."

That does not mean that he did not follow cricket, and Hampshire in particular, very closely after he retired from playing the game. "I wouldn't miss an evening paper and I would go straight to the Hampshire score and see what they were doing. If I'd have lived in Hampshire I would have liked to have taken a more active part, like being on the cricket committee or something, if they'd asked me. It is very difficult if you're living in London, to have a place on a committee which you feel is slightly ex-officio because they've got to give it to you. And I would have wanted to play an active part by making a realistic contribution, which I was really not able to do."

Having set a precedent by winning the County Championship title in 1961, Ingleby-Mackenzie could take pleasure from afar when Hampshire went on being successful, and there was no greater pleasure for him than when Richard Gilliat lifted the title once again in 1973. "This was quite interesting, because everybody said it must be pretty galling for you because you won it the first time ever, and now Richard Gilliat has won it. I no more thought it was a pity than jump over the moon, because I was thrilled that Richard won the Championship. We put a marker on the map in 1961, in that we could win the competition, and he then went on to win in 1973. I congratulated him and it was absolutely superb. One-day competitions are fine, but to me the Championship is the pinnacle, the absolute jewel in the crown."

Others looking on at how Ingleby-Mackenzie and his team played their cricket always commented on the charisma of the man and the fun and enjoyment to be seen on the field. Was that a summary of his philosophy about the game? "I don't know about charisma because I'm just myself, but certainly fun and enjoyment are absolutely vital. I think you can display your own prowess on the cricket field, and sometimes you do better than others, but there's no deception as to whether you're enjoying the game and having fun. I certainly did, right the way through my career, and I think it's infectious to the crowd. I think if you're enjoying it they enjoy it with you."

Colin Ingleby-Mackenzie later served as president of the MCC, which voted during his term and with his encouragement to allow the election of women members to the famous club. He died from a malignant brain tumour in March 2006 at the age of 72. All that can be said of one who passes at such a relatively young age is that it was a good job he packed so much into the years he did have. The crowd, and everyone whose life he touched, certainly enjoyed it with him.

Brian Statham
1930–2000

Brian Statham

OVER THE YEARS THERE *have been some great fast bowling partnerships, but most of those which readily come to mind are from overseas. Lindwall and Miller, Hall and Griffith, Lillee and Thomson; but there is one English pair who definitely rank alongside the very best—Statham and Trueman. Brian Statham was the Lancashire component in that Roses partnership, and while the Yorkshire element might have stolen many of the more outrageous headlines, it was Brian Statham who perhaps was the "cricketer's cricketer". Fast but above all accurate, "If the batsmen misses, I'll hit" was a motto which served him, Lancashire and England supremely well.*

John Brian Statham was born in Manchester in 1930, made his Lancashire debut in 1950, and the following winter was in action for England in New Zealand. He continued to grace the Test scene until 1965, playing in 70 matches and taking 252 wickets at under 23 apiece. His record in all first-class cricket provided the backbone of the Lancashire attack up to 1968, when he retired with 2,260 wickets at only 16.36 each. He captained Lancashire between 1965 and 1967, and was awarded the CBE for his services to cricket.

While he was famed for his partnership with Fred Trueman, he was probably at his peak in 1954/55, in Australia with Frank Tyson, and it was said that he was only a little bit below Tyson's pace at that time. "It was quite a bit in actual fact. Frank is probably the quickest bowler I've ever seen. Day in, day out, on the English scene, it was probably Fred, but for a very short period Frank was very, very fast indeed. I preferred to bowl with Fred. Fred knew exactly what he was about. He was a very professional cricketer. He knew his job and he got on with it, and he was tremendously strong, but not as strong as some of his captains thought. There were occasions when Fred was overbowled, and occasions when I was overbowled. That's part and parcel of the game. Fred and I were in many ways perfect foils for each other. Fred had the ability to make the ball swing. I didn't move the ball much in the air, but I moved it off the wicket. Fred's line could stray a little bit, trying to bowl outswingers; I relied purely on accuracy and length."

There was usually more than adequate support at the other end for Statham in Tests, but was that the case with Lancashire? "Well in the early days I had no support whatsoever really. I opened the bowling with many people, including Malcolm Hilton, Roy Tattersall, Peter Greenwood, but nobody quick. It wasn't really until Ken Higgs came on to the scene that I had a genuine partner. Ken wasn't the paciest of opening bowlers, but he had tremendous strength and didn't mind which end he bowled at, which was fine for me because I could bowl downwind now and again, which was rather nice."

Back in the early days, where did Statham's association with cricket begin? "I played cricket from primary school days. We were very fortunate. I went to a school called Aspinal School in Gorton, and they were probably the only primary school in Manchester that had their own grass cricket pitch, which was very nice. So I was playing cricket there from the age of, something like seven I suppose and always as a quick bowler."

Although having an advantage by playing cricket at primary school, he did not see any county cricket and so there were no role models for the budding fast bowler. "I always wanted to play rather than to watch. I didn't even read about it in the papers. Until 1949 I really knew nothing at all about county cricket, or the players playing in it. The interest in cricket came from playing. Whilst I was doing national service there was a boy called Larry Lazarus, who was secretary for the camp I was stationed at. He was a Middlesex member, and he saw me bowl and asked whether I'd ever thought about playing county cricket, which of course I hadn't, and in actual fact he wrote to Middlesex for a trial, and they referred him back to Lancashire, me being Lancashire-born.

"When I'd left school I played for a little club called Denton West, in the then North Western League, which has subsequently finished. But several of us went from a soccer team so there was a group of five or six of us went to this club, and I was fortunate enough to play for the first team, the first season I went. So I was thrown in the deep end from the start, and it seems to have been my fortune, or misfortune, to have been thrown in the deep end many times."

For the young Statham there was not the luxury, or handicap, of coaching. He had a natural, if slightly unorthodox action, and relied on natural ability, of which there was plenty. "I had a modicum of coaching at Old Trafford under Stan Worthington, but I got into the county side so quickly that coaching only lasted for six or seven weeks I suppose. I've always counted myself very fortunate that a coach didn't get hold of me. I think any coach could have ruined what I was able to do. I hadn't a purist action by any stretch of the imagination. One is always taught from the purist and the coaching books that you look round the outside of your left arm. I didn't. I looked underneath it, but I kept looking, and it certainly didn't do me any harm."

So where did the phenomenal accuracy come from? "Purely con-centration, I've always felt. Looking at what you're trying to hit, and concentrating on it, like a dart thrower. You're not liable to hit it unless you're looking at it, and I think it was purely con-centration."

It was said that there was a pattern on the pitch at the end of a day's play, when he had been bowling for some time, which was often likened to a bull's-eye with the shots just around it, because he generally hit the same spot. "Well, I'll take your word for that! I never bothered to look, to be honest. At the end of an innings I was only too pleased to get off and get my feet up."

Having got onto the Lancashire staff at Old Trafford, who were the other players in the side at that time? "Washbrook, Ikin, Grieves, Jeff Edrich, Alan Wharton, Malcolm Hilton, Roy Tattersall, the wicket-keeper at the time was Alf Barlow, and there were lads like Peter Greenwood around, Bob Berry. It was a pretty good side, and a very fine fielding side close to the wicket."

The fact that he was thrown in at the deep end, as he said, into the Lancashire side, meant that he did not have a long-seated ambition to be a professional cricketer. "No, I'd no ambitions towards being a professional cricketer at all. I came to watch Lancashire play Middlesex in 1949, and it was a beautiful summer's day. Middlesex were batting, Edrich and Compton were in the middle of a season when they got a lot of runs. Jack Robertson and Bill Brown opened the innings, they both got centuries. Compton came in and played a typical swashbuckling innings, dancing down the wicket and hitting the ball here, there and everywhere, and I thought, I wonder what the devil I'm getting myself into? All these runs being scored; I mean in the cricket I'd been accustomed to, 150 was a large score and there were these guys, I think they were 350 at teatime or something, and I thought, well, this is a long day. However, we'll have a go and see what it's all about."

Asked if that was one of the first county matches he had seen, Statham replied that that was the only county match he'd ever seen! Even the trial that was organised for him the following spring was washed out, but he did not mind too much because he had obtained a special leave pass from the RAF to attend. In fact, he enjoyed some good cricket while in the services. "The camp cricket was quite good. We visited various camps and played different commands. Some of the cricket was of a reasonably high standard, I suppose minor counties standard, but I thoroughly enjoyed what cricket I played in the RAF."

While he was watching the Middlesex batsmen stroke the ball around Old Trafford with ease, did he wonder what he had let himself in for, and have any doubts that he was going to make it? "I suppose I must have had. I was a very slight boy. I should think I was under 11 stone at the time, and at six foot high that makes you pretty slim. And of course my cricket was of four hours' duration, two of which you'd spend in the field, more or less, and you'd done an awful lot of bowling. It was one of the situations where the captain put you on at one end and more or less forgot you until the innings was finished. A bit like the pros in the league, there is a tendency for captains to put them on at one end, and that's where they stay until the match is finished."

He was slight of build, which led to his nickname. "The Whippet, the Gorton Greyhound. That's relating to Bellevue greyhound track, where I was born in Gorton. Yes, I was very slight."

He was also known as George, for some reason. "There always seemed to have been a George in the Lancashire side, and

Winston Place was affectionately known as George, and when
Winston retired I seemed to take it over."

He made his first-class debut for Lancashire on his 20th birthday
against Kent at Old Trafford, an event he recalled clearly. "I
always remember Cyril Washbrook, as we were walking down
onto the ground. We lost the toss so we were in the field; those
were in the days when if one won the toss one batted, you didn't
even think about putting the opposition in. I remember Cyril
saying, 'This chap Arthur Fagg, whatever you do don't bowl short
to him, he's one of the finest hookers playing, and if you bowl
short at him he'll hook you out of sight.' So I said, 'Oh, thank you
very much.' So away we go and I started bowling, and dropped
one short to this bloke, who tried to hook it and it was a little
quicker than he thought and hit the splice, and he was caught at
mid-wicket by Alan Wharton. So Cyril came strolling across
whilst the other batsman was coming in, and said, 'I thought I told
you not to bowl short to Arthur Fagg.' I said, 'Yes, but you didn't
tell me who Arthur Fagg was!' And I'd really no idea. I'd no idea
of any of the players. I really didn't even know the players I was
playing with, never mind the players I was playing against."

There was no chance of him being overawed by bowling to
batsmen with great reputations. On the other hand, they had no
idea who he was, so it must have come as something of a shock
when this slight young lad came running in and propelled the
ball with great pace and accuracy. "I think it probably did, but
I was so inexperienced and they were talking about outswingers,
inswingers, off-spinners, slow left-arm and leg-spinners and
googlies and I didn't know what on earth they were talking
about. I was really that raw."

That meant that he had to learn, and learn quickly, from the
other professionals, acquiring his craft on the job. "We talked

about the game an awful lot in those days, and really the conversation in the evening was all about cricket. Really from April to September, that's basically all we talked about. Cricket, not necessarily the game we were playing in, but things about the game in general. I think that some of the soundest advice I ever received was from Harry Makepeace, and he said, 'Always be prepared to be a good listener. You can learn nothing with your mouth, you can learn an awful lot with your ears. Things you hear, you pick the things out that are going to be of benefit to you. If there is a load of rubbish being talked, well, listen and forget it.'"

Statham never swung the ball very much, but he obtained movement off the seam in either direction. "Well, this is so, yes. If the ball really swung, I was in trouble, because the direction went. The whole of my theory was based on length and direction."

It was a philosophy that led to his famous catchphrase of "If they miss, I'll hit", a phrase that he developed himself. To acquire this consistency, did he do much training and practice? "Practice and training?! Training, no. Practice, once the season had started, very, very little in actual fact, a few minutes in the morning before the game, but that was all once the season had started. Pre-season practice was very intense. I would bowl for the best part of four hours a day, two hours in the morning and two hours in the afternoon. This bowling was going to tone up all the muscles I was going to use doing exactly that, bowling. I was cricket fit, and our seasons were very much tougher in terms of workload than they are today.

"You had to learn to pace your day. You knew exactly what you were going to be doing for the next four months once you started, and that was three-day cricket, so everything was similar day by day. You weren't messing about with one-day games stuck in between three-day games or four-day games. We had a better grounding than they get today for Championship cricket."

He remarked how it did not take long before he was suddenly whisked into the Lancashire team. It was an equally short apprenticeship in county cricket before he found himself playing Test cricket. "Well, that's quite right. I played four, five or six weeks with the second team. I think I only played three or four games with them, made the county side and never appeared with the second team again. Those were the only matches I played with the second team, which I suppose is a bit unusual, and then by January I found myself in Australia, again not knowing the players I was going to play with, or the players I was going to play against, which is a most peculiar situation, and I suppose a bit unnerving."

He had played just 15 first-class matches by the end of the 1950 season, taking 37 wickets at just 16.56 apiece. So when the England touring party in Australia needed a replacement quick, Statham was flown out to join the party. "They'd lost a lot of bowlers through injury. I think John Warr was one of the few who was remaining fit. I think Trevor Bailey had broken down; Alec Bedser wasn't as fit as he ought to be. I think John Warr and Freddie Brown were opening the bowling at the time. I flew out on 4th January 1951, and arrived there about 8th January. We flew into Sydney in a thunderstorm and had to fly to Melbourne to get some practice, it rained that hard in Sydney! Most extraordinary."

He did not get to play in a Test match in Australia, and failed to pull up any trees in the two state matches in which he appeared. He was not particularly successful against Auckland at the start of the New Zealand leg of the tour, but a good performance against Otago got him into the side for the first Test. "I don't remember a lot about it. I got a wicket, but it really was like a dream. It seemed very unreal then, and it seems very unreal now. Not quite sure whether it happened or not—you know, that sort of situation. I enjoyed it but it was very hard for me. The heat was quite intense at that time, in January in Australia. The first match we played was an up-country game at a place called Renmark in Victoria, and it was 102 degrees. We then arrive in Adelaide, and it's just a shade hotter, about 105, and I played my first first-class game out there, against South Australia, and the ball wouldn't bounce much more than an inch or two above the bails, and it was the flattest wicket I'd ever seen in my life, and of course no grass on it. Very difficult. Then we flew across to New Zealand, by flying boat, would you believe?"

He returned from that trip as a Test bowler, so did that make a difference to how he was treated when he reported for duty back at Old Trafford at the start of the 1951 season? "No, not at all! A Test bowler with one match's experience? I'd only played in a few first-class games in 1950, so overall I wouldn't have had more than 20 first-class matches under my belt at the start of my second season."

But he did enough then to stay in the Test side for a long and distinguished career. "In and out, yes, in England. I played most of the matches when I toured, but I was very in and out in England."

Asked what sort of a second season he had for Lancashire, he replied: "No idea. I haven't a clue! Pretty good, I think."

It was pretty good, with 97 wickets at 15.11, but he was not a records man. "No, I'm not, no! I've never been one for facts and figures, no."

But what about more tangible mementos? Did he collect stumps that he hit in Test matches that he played in, and keep balls with which he took significant wickets? "I've got some of the balls; I've got some of the stumps. I've never done anything with the stumps. I suppose I've got seven or eight stumps, and never known what to do with them. I've no doubt my grandson will end up with them—he'll probably play with them."

Did he regard cricket as a sort of job of work, or did it have a magic of its own for him? "It was really a way of life, as much as anything. I never regarded it purely as a job. It was a great, fun way to earn a living, and that's all it was in those days, earning a living, not earning a lot of money. And Lancashire were a fun side to be with. They were a great crowd of lads, and always have been. Really over the last 40 years they've been a great crowd of lads."

In those days, especially, they were a side with quite a few characters around. "Oh yes, yes indeed. Alf Barlow, the first wicket-keeper I played with, he was quite a character. He'd been a rear gunner during the war, and had a lot of anecdotes about the war days, great fun. I remember he was talking to a group of schoolboys here. We had schoolboys down for Easter coaching, and these boys were saying, 'Were you in the war, Mr Barlow?' And he said, 'Yes, I was in the war, I was a flyer, I was a rear gunner.' 'And did you fly a lot?' they said. 'Fly a lot?' he said. 'They only let me down for meals!'"

There must have been times when he was bowling for Lancashire that he thought they only took him off for meals, because he did have long, long stints. "Yes, a normal day would be to bowl for the first hour, or if things were going well even a little longer than the first hour, and there would always be two overs, three overs just before lunch, which was quite sufficient to ruin my lunch! I would start off immediately after lunch for 50 minutes, or an hour. We would then be looking for the second new ball, but you would have a bit of a loosener directly after tea, then perhaps one over before the new ball, and then it depended on how things went, how long you bowled then."

After that first brief tour of Australia and New Zealand, he went on tours all over the world. Which was his favourite destination? "We always enjoyed going to Australia, that was always regarded as the premier trip. The cricket was hard, but the fun was good, it was a nice place to visit. South Africa was a great tour to make."

On his next trip to Australia in 1954/55, it was said that he was probably at his peak, but did he feel that he was? "Yes, I probably was. I was 24, 25 then, and hardened to the stresses and strains of county cricket, which physically are quite hard. But as I said earlier, you learn to pace your day, you know pretty well from the start of the day how the day is going to go for you, and you learn how to make yourself last, to have something left at the end of the day. And as I previously said, the 30 three-day games was a great grounding for learning how to pace the day. The '54 trip, I think I only played seven games on the trip, five of which were Test matches, and a couple of state games and one or two two-day up-country games, but they were very hard matches, and low-scoring matches are always a bit hard on the nerves, you have to keep control of yourself and keep things going. I didn't have choice of ends; Leonard Hutton gave Frank the choice of ends, which was invariably downhill and downwind, so I had the other end to contend with, but we did very well as a team, Frank and I."

It must have been a happy trip as well, because the side was so successful. "Happy after the first Test, yes, the first Test was not an enjoyable occasion! When Leonard won the toss and put

Australia in to bat, basically on the assumption that the wicket was going to be as quick as it had been in the state game, and of course when we went out on the first morning and tried this thing out, there was no pace in it at all, and I got a wicket after some 20 minutes or so, and that was the only wicket I got. I ended up with one for 130-odd in a lot of overs, and Australia made 600 and plenty I think it was, and we lost by an innings and 200-plus. Not a very happy match.

"With the side that had been selected to play in that Test match, I don't think Len had any option but to put the opposition in. He'd played all the fast bowlers, and really no back-up bowling at all, so everything was much of a muchness. I suppose it was very like the make-up of the West Indies side. You had enough bowlers to keep going for the day, but everything was the same, you changed one bowler for another like bowler. We never played the four quick bowlers again. Frank shortened his run-up, his rhythm improved tremendously, and his accuracy improved out of all recognition. He suddenly started bowling straight, with no lack of pace, and he made the ball bounce.

"Frank kept it going for a long, long time. He bowled long spells. We both bowled long spells, but his pace really was fantastic and the Australians didn't like it one bit, and the number of times that you saw the bottom hand being taken off the bat, they were doing it three or four times an over. They didn't like it at all, and they certainly didn't like the bouncers."

When he came back from Australia there was more hard work. Against South Africa at Lord's in 1955, he bowled for something like three and three-quarter hours in one spell, and got his best Test return. "Yes, overall in the innings I bowled for 29 overs straight. I bowled at the pavilion end all the way through the innings, but that took place over two days. We had a spell of rain on the morning of the second day in the field, which broke it up a little, but I did do a long, long stint, that's quite right, but that was of my own choosing. This was not the captain's fault, this was my fault. I suddenly got it into my mind that I could bowl them out. Well, I knew I could bowl them out, I had the confidence to bowl them out, and the ball was moving around for me, and I thought I'd like to bowl through the innings, and did just that."

He finished with seven for 39. "That's right. But I was very pleased to see Johnny Wardle get a couple of wickets at the other end, I really was! I was pleased when it was all over."

But what sort of state was he in when he went back to Lancashire for county matches after a spell like that? "Not very good. I'd strained a stomach muscle in actual fact, doing it. So I think I missed the next match, but there is always a feeling of anti-climax leaving a Test match and going back to the county, and it really can take an hour or two to pull yourself together and get stuck in again. But they're the bread and butter, yes indeed, and I always felt it was as important to do your best for your county side as it was to do it for England, for the country side."

He certainly did do it, on a number of occasions, finishing up with a record 1,816 wickets for Lancashire, and in 1957 he also got his best analysis of eight for 34, 15 for 89 in a match against Warwickshire. Did he remember that one? "Yes, it was at Courtaulds in Coventry. I got 50 runs in that match as well, so I regarded myself as the pro for the match! The ball wobbled about all over the place there, and I think Cyril Washbrook got a lot of runs in that match."

So was the pitch a bit more treacherous than just wobbling about? "No, it purely moved off the seam. The bounce was all right, perhaps they didn't bat too well."

A lot of people did not bat awfully well against him, because there were a crowd of county batsmen who were not too keen on getting behind the line when he was bowling. "Leicester were one of those sides. I always enjoyed playing at Grace Road. I always had to work very hard, but I always had something to show at the end of the day. I always reckoned on 10 wickets at Leicester."

In fact, he got one of his three first-class hat-tricks against Leicester, in 1958. "I believe you. I know one was Sussex, and I know one was at Johannesburg. I know that in Johannesburg they were all bowled, and I thought it was off stump, middle stump, leg stump. I could be wrong about that, but I know they were all bowled, and that Peter Heine was one of them."

He developed this famous reputation with Fred Trueman, but it was often Trueman who took the limelight. People seemed to focus on him—Fiery Fred—and at the other end Brian Statham bowled and bowled and bowled. Was he ever aware of this imbalance in publicity? "Yes, I was, but I really shunned publicity, I wasn't interested in publicity. All I wanted to do was to get out there and do the job I was paid to do. The rest of it I could comfortably do without. I didn't like publicity, I genuinely did shun it. Fred was a different character altogether. He really thought that even bad news was better than no news. But Fred was a great performer, make no mistake. He was a great bowler, and one didn't have to tell Fred which batsmen you wanted down at your end, nor did he have to do tell me which batsmen he fancied, and we worked in tandem extremely well together. We shared many meals together, many pints together over the years, but we thoroughly enjoyed playing together, really did."

They got on as individuals, because there are several instances of such partnerships in public life that do not exist in private; they

*are purely professional partnerships. But that was not the case
with Statham and Trueman, because they were genuinely mates.*
"We've never had a cross word in 40 years, and I mean that.
Never once. I did once throw a punch at him, but we'd had a few
beers and I'd gone to bed early, and left the cooling system on
full blast. I was lying on top of the bed in just a pair of
underpants, going a very deep blue, when Fred walked in the
room and very gently tried to put a blanket over me, and I
thought I was being robbed and took a swing at him.
Fortunately I missed, or he'd have broken my back. He did
threaten to do that if I did it again! That was in Guyana, which
was very hot and very humid, and the ground there is actually
eight or nine feet below sea level, which must be unique within
the game, I think, but it is a very sultry place. We did a little test
there, in actual fact, about weight loss, and I actually lost four
pounds in one day in the field in Guyana, and put it back on
overnight. I was exactly the same on the second day as I'd
started off on the first day."

*He had a spell as Lancashire captain, between 1965 and 1967,
which was reported as a very well-organised spell. Did he enjoy
captaincy?* "No, I didn't. Quick bowling is too physically
demanding to do a good job as a captain. The only job I could
do, basically, was to hold youngsters together, and try and teach
them how to play the game, and what the game was all about.
One got too tired to think about who had bowled, and particularly in the one-day games. We'd only got the Gillette Cup in
those days, that was from 1965 to '68, and of course that was
slotted in with a full county season. I did find it very difficult to
remember who had bowled and how many they'd bowled, and
try and juggle them, and really Jackie Bond and some of the
other boys helped me out tremendously during those matches.
We were really not *au fait* with the manner in which to play
these games. I detested running up to bowl with only the wicket-

keeper stood there, and the batsmen in between. Everything was visually wrong for me, and I didn't enjoy running up to bowl with the object of saving runs rather than taking wickets, that was completely alien to me.

"I managed in the Championship all right. Possibly a tendency to overbowl yourself a little, which was probably wrong because there were kids around at the time who needed the experience, lads like Ken Shuttleworth, Peter Lever, just getting into the side really, and perhaps they should have shared some of the responsibilities, some of the brunt of the workload. I was getting too old for it anyway!"

The year he began his term as captain of Lancashire was also the year when he was recalled to the England side. "Yes, I was. Very surprising, for the last Test South Africa played here before isolation, which was at the Oval. It was very nice, because Ken Higgs was selected as well, and that was Ken Higgs' first Test match and my last Test match, and I think if I'm right we shared 15 wickets between us."

He took five for 40 in the first innings, and that took him up to 250 Test wickets, only the second bowler to achieve the milestone after Trueman. Trueman went on for a few more years, but for Statham it was a return to county cricket. Did he miss the stimulus of Test cricket? "No, not at all. At 35, for a quick bowler, you really are too old. From the age of 30, basically, your pace is diminishing, you're not going to get any quicker once you've reached the age of 30, and it's physically very demanding. You'll always get through the first day in the field all right, but it's the next day, and if your team's batting should fail, and you've got to go into the field again, it's very hard, very hard."

*Statham celebrates claiming his 250th Test wicket, that of
South Africa's 'Tiger' Lance at the Oval in 1965*

He mentioned a game in which he got 50. He did not have too many opportunities to use his left-handed batting abilities. Did he, like most bowlers, and quick bowlers in particular, enjoy the opportunities when they came? "To a degree. I must say that particularly in the early part of my career, we were not really encouraged to bat long. Our job was to bowl, and as soon as you were out you were going to be bowling, ten minutes later more or less, so they didn't encourage you to lose too much time out there. If you were going to get runs they wanted them got quickly, and they didn't want any loss of energy. I remember when I made my highest score, which was also against Leicester. I can't remember the bowler, but he kept bowling vaguely short at me, and I was literally baseballing him over mid-wicket, and I got 62 in 23 minutes. There was a hundred quid for the fastest hundred in those days, and I suddenly thought, 'I could win a hundred quid here,' and then a wicket fell and somebody came in and said, 'Skipper says get out, now.' So I hacked all the wickets down and got out. Cyril said, 'Sorry about that. I wanted to declare, and I'm going to bat on for ten minutes, plus the ten minutes. That gives you 20 minutes' break,' which happened and I think I ended up with four wickets that night, so I was quite satisfied with the day."

He was noted as being an outstanding professional, and the story about that innings underlines the fact. When he was told to get out, he got out. He was always a very unobtrusive character, unemotional, some might say. Was that by design, or just the way he was? "It's just the way I am, really. I'm a pretty placid person. I like to do basic things well, and I think perhaps it's one of the departments that isn't looked into closely enough today. I think perhaps some of the people playing are not paying enough attention to the basics, getting the basics absolutely right, and they're missing out because of that."

That is a philosophy of professional pride, but if the batsmen nicked him through the slips without it going to hand, or it just shaved the stumps, did he show excitement on the field, or did he just go back to his mark and carry on bowling? "It would always have appeared on the face of it that I just went back to the mark and got on with it. There were words said within me that do not bear repeating! I always felt for the bloke who'd dropped it or the bloke who'd missed it, because it never happens on purpose, and nobody feels worse than the bloke who's been unfortunate enough to misfield, or miss a catch."

So did he ever remember losing his temper on the cricket field? "Yes, I can. Oddly enough we are going back to Guyana again, and an incident involving Denis Compton, who was not at his fittest. His knees were not particularly good, and Denis was fielding at third slip, I think it was. I'd just got a wicket, and a bloke called Clifford McWatt came in, who was the wicket-keeper and a left-hander. I'd had a very long spell, and I'd had enough, and I knew Len was going to give me the sweater, even though I'd just taken a wicket, and I said, 'Just one more, please, skipper, I fancy this bloke. If he's down this end, would you let me have another go at him?' So he shook his head and mumbled, 'All right then, see who's down there.' And he happened to be down that end, and I think it was about the second ball of the over, lovely thick outside edge, straight to Denis, knee height. Denis held one knee together with one hand and tried to catch it with the other, and put the thing down, and I really was annoyed, and sort of snatched the sweater at the end of the over and said, 'That's me finished,' and Denis knew it. And Denis recalls the incident quite frequently, I'm given to understand!"

Was that the only time? "I got very annoyed once in the West Indies. I think Fred had been bowling at one end, and it was just before lunch, and he hit the opening bat on the glove and he was caught at short leg. The opening bat immediately started rubbing his elbow, and got away with it, and then had the audacity to come into our dressing room to ask for treatment from our physiotherapist on his fingers, during the luncheon interval. And then the West Indian skipper, I've forgotten who it was, asked if we minded if somebody else went in after lunch while this bloke went for an X-ray on his fingers, which we thought was unkind. Fred said, 'I'm going to have him after lunch,' and I said, 'Well if you don't, I will!' Fred didn't manage to get him down his end, but he got down my end, and I hit him first ball under the heart, which really I've regretted ever since. I wanted to scare the daylights out of him, I didn't want to hit the bloke, but as it happened I did, and he went down in a heap, spitting blood, and I really didn't enjoy the incident very much, but it's very vivid in my mind."

He got the wicket, shortly afterwards. But it appears that he was the antithesis of all we are led to believe a quick bowler should be. They should be aggressive, flamboyant, and he was quiet, retiring? "Oh yes. I was very shy, basically. To a degree I still am, I suppose, but I was a very retiring, shy boy."

When he finished playing, he did not lose contact with Lancashire, because he was elected to the committee. Did he enjoy that aspect of the game? "I've always enjoyed my association with Lancashire, yes. I don't suppose there's an awful lot we can do on committee, the ex-players, these days, because cricket is basically run by the captains and the cricket manager, and to a large degree I agree with that being so. We do have contracts meetings and this sort of thing, but I can't say that those are meetings that any of the old players enjoy. It's no fun deciding whether you're going to give a contract or let a boy go, which is, in effect, firing him. Nobody likes to sack another player."

What about when it came to giving help and advice to a later crop of quick bowlers? Was he ever asked to do that? "Very rarely, very rarely indeed. Daffy DeFreitas asked questions, Peter Martin also asked questions. Paul Allott did once, but apart from them, nobody."

Did he regret that? "Well, I think I could have had long chats with these people and told them what I thought, and given them the benefit of my experience. I don't profess to be a coach, but the basic principles are still the same as they always were, and I'm sure they would have learned something."

The key to fast bowling for him was simple. "It's purely length and direction. You achieve that with concentration. And I would tell anybody to learn to do the simple things well, learn the basics well."

And it did not matter to him what sort of action a bowler had, as long as he could achieve that? "Not at all, no. I was watching an old film of Ray Lindwall bowling, and I suppose my memory isn't as good as it should be, but I hadn't realised how low Ray's arm was. From that film he was almost a slinger, not that there's anything against that, but Ray had magnificent control over length, direction and swing. He controlled the ball beautifully, and of course Leslie Jackson from Derbyshire was very much a slinger. Very different action from Ray Lindwall, but his arm looked roughly about the same height. But Ray was a superb bowler."

He had remarked how he always liked to shun the limelight, but a couple of years earlier some of his ex-colleagues got together, with Fred Trueman to the fore, and organised a benefit occasion for him. "Yes, they did. It was a very nice occasion. A little bit embarrassing I suppose, and a bit awe-inspiring. It was a dinner attended by some 1,000 people. One, it was a very large room, and two, Fred and I appeared down a staircase to a bank of trumpeters, which was a bit off-putting to say the least! That's not my style at all, no! And then I had to make a very important speech at the end of it, which I really didn't look forward to, to be honest, and I made sure I was very sober when I got up to do it. I wasn't very sober afterwards, but at the time I got up to speak I was very sober!"

Trueman was awarded the OBE in 1989, while Statham received the CBE in 1966; it could have been the one instance of Statham getting choice of ends! "Yes, this is so. Fred was delighted with his honour, and I was equally delighted with mine. I really basically can't understand why I should have received a higher honour than Fred, because Fred put the same amount of work in as I did, perhaps even more. He took more Test wickets than I did, and was equally as loyal to his county as any other player. He was very loyal Yorkshire, Fred, extremely loyal."

Did Statham remember the day he went to the Palace for the investiture? "Yes, I do. I remember the day, and my two—then—small boys were with me. In fact that was rather amusing, because we'd had to hurry and scuffle about, all getting changed and getting down to the Palace in good time, and from getting inside the Palace to the thing actually taking place, we seemed to have been in there a week before anything started happening. My wife, Audrey, told me that they very kindly put her and the boys on the front row, where the boys could see everything. And then a lady tapped her on the shoulder and said, 'I hope you don't mind, but your little boy has his flies undone,' which she said was awfully embarrassing at the time! Peter had been walking about the Palace with his flies undone!"

Statham professed to be poor with dates and facts and figures, but all Lancashire followers remember the dates 1950 to 1968, the years when he graced the Old Trafford scene, and played such an important part in Lancashire cricket. "For myself, I thoroughly enjoyed it. I would do it all over again in exactly the same way. I really had a ball here, it was great fun, I made many lifelong friends. It really was super; I've enjoyed it very much."

It was probably only opposing batsmen who did not enjoy themselves when Brian "George" Statham was around. His popularity was acknowledged when he was made president of Lancashire in 1997, while his loss from leukaemia in 2000, just before his 70th birthday, was as keenly felt as any cricketing death.

Denis Compton
1918–1997

Denis Compton

O VER ALL THE YEARS *that cricket has been played, there has been a very select band of men who have become, in the modern idiom, cult figures. W.G. Grace was perhaps the first, Don Bradman should certainly be included, and there is an argument for Ian Botham to be added to the ranks. Denis Compton, however you like to measure eligibility, must surely be included. The word charisma could have been coined just to describe the appeal of Denis Charles Scott Compton in post-war Britain. Whether scoring runs with a distinctive style, discussing the state of the Compton knee, or smiling out from advertisements, Denis Compton was never out of the public spotlight.*

Born at Hendon in 1918, he made his Middlesex debut in 1936 and for his county, for England, and in India, where he played cricket during the war, he scored 38,942 first-class runs, at an average of 51.85, with 123 centuries. He also took 622 wickets at only 32.27, and he held 415 catches. In his 78 Tests, he maintained an average of over 50, for his 5,807 runs, with 17 centuries. Yet it is not figures, not even figures as good as those, which still bring a smile to the face of anyone who can remember seeing Denis Compton play cricket. He was, quite simply, a batting genius. But where were the seeds of that genius planted?

"At school I loved the game of cricket and football, but I suppose my career really started when I came here to Lord's at the age of 14. I was selected to play for the elementary schools against the public schools, and fortunately I managed to get a hundred. There happened to be a certain gentleman here who was terribly important to cricket in those days, Sir Pelham Warner, and he was responsible for bringing me on to the Lord's ground staff."

It is not always the case that much cricket was played in schools, but Compton could number the schoolmasters among the influential figures who impacted on his embryonic career. "The schoolmasters at my school and many others in the Hendon district were all great enthusiasts for the game of cricket, and we had a very competitive number of schools that played. I should think we played two or three school games a week. But I had a lot of enthusiastic supporters. Number one, I think, was my father. He was marvellous, and he was a club cricketer himself, but he encouraged me to play sport throughout, and then a number of masters, Mark Mitchell and Mr Bond, were both tremendously keen on both soccer and cricket, and they encouraged me. In fact, Mark Mitchell said to my father one day, 'I think this boy's going to be a sportsman. Unfortunately he's not going to be an academic!'

With that sort of background, did he have any thoughts other than becoming a professional sportsman? "I didn't, but my mother did. At first, when I was asked to come on the ground staff, my mother said, 'No, I'm afraid not, because that's only four months of the year. What's the boy going to do for the next eight?' And she said, 'I preferably would like to see him become a civil servant, and start in the town hall at Hendon.' But then I played an international for England schoolboys, and one of the Arsenal scouts happened to be there, and he came to my father and mother and said, 'We would like to take him onto the staff at Arsenal.' So my mother then said, 'Oh well, I'll have to agree with father, that's the other eight months, so he's now fully occupied for 12 months!'

*The fact that his elder brother, Leslie, was playing for Arsenal,
and played for Middlesex, presumably eased the way, or was he
spotted first?* "No, my brother got spotted first. In fact, I used
to be cleaning the stands when he was training as a professional for Arsenal. He was a good chap, my brother Leslie, very
encouraging and very nice indeed. Far from being jealous of my
success, he was the other way. It gave him almost as much
pleasure for me to score runs, and score goals, as himself, or
more pleasure to see me do all these things. There was a lovely
atmosphere. Leslie was a marvellous footballer, and surprisingly enough for a man of six feet two or three, he was a very
capable wicket-keeper too, and not a bad batsman; a very
useful player."

*How much first-class cricket did he see before he started playing
himself?* "I saw quite a lot when I came and joined the staff,
although I do vividly remember my father bringing me to Lord's

*Compton in action as Arsenal's outside-left against Bolton Wanderers
at Highbury in 1950*

in 1930, to see the great Don Bradman play, and we came on the Friday night, and Test matches then used to start on a Saturday. He brought the camp bed, and I slept outside the ground at the Nursery end. You had to do that, otherwise you couldn't get in to see the Australians, and so I got in on Saturday morning and saw him make, I think it was 183—fantastic—and little did I think that I was going to be playing against him in 1938."

So Bradman was one of his early heroes. Were there others? "Oh yes, but particularly Jack Hobbs. I loved him, and in fact I was a Surrey supporter, because of my adoration for Jack Hobbs of Surrey. My father took me down to see him play, and it wasn't Jack who succeeded, I think he only got 22 runs, but Andy Sandham I saw make about 162. It was on an August bank holiday Monday. Surrey played Notts, but I also saw Jack score his 300 runs at Lord's, and Patsy Hendren I loved. Bradman of course was the greatest batsmen I've ever seen. Wally Hammond, a marvellous all-rounder, and Leslie Ames, a lovely man. I didn't try and model myself on any of them. I just played as I played, naturally. I just went out, and I really didn't know how I played. I know many people said to me, 'How did you hold the bat?' I said, 'Well get me a bat and I'll show you, I couldn't tell you how I held it.' I never used to work it out theoretically."

At that time he was looking at these great players from the outside, and then suddenly, and it was fairly sudden, he found himself playing alongside them, and against them. Was there any feeling of awe, or did he settle very quickly into the first-class game? "There was a feeling of awe, yes. I mean it was a wonderful feeling for me, to think that I was actually playing against cricketers who were my idols when I was a schoolboy. I loved it, and of course I suppose one of my greatest thrills ever, even to the end of my career, was being selected for my first match, for Middlesex against Sussex at Whitsun, and I was picked as a bowler. I batted number 11, and I know we wanted something like 30 to secure a first-innings lead, which was very important in those days. I arrived at the wicket, and of course at the other end was the great Sir Gubby Allen. We made the 30 runs, and I never forget that we got what we wanted, but Jim Parks was the bowler, and I was given out LBW. An umpire called Bill Reeves, a wonderful character indeed, gave me out, and I remember Gubby turning to him, and saying, 'Oh, Bill, you are a bloody cheat, that little boy wasn't LBW!' He said, 'Oh I know, sir, but he's going to be OK, and I was dying for a wee!'

He never batted at number 11 again, but slowly worked his way up the order until he settled at four, where he stayed for the rest of his career. It was as a batsman that he was generally remembered but, as over 600 wickets would testify, he was a more than useful bowler. "I loved bowling. I started by being left-arm orthodox, and then suddenly I found that rather dull, and then one day I met a very great Australian bowler who played for Leicester, called Jack Walsh. He said to me, 'Denis, if you want a bit of fun, why don't you try and bowl what I do, these chinamen, googlies,' and I said, 'I don't think I'd know how.' He took me to the nets, showed me how it was done, and I did a little bit of practice with it, and thought, 'Ooh, this is fun!' And that's really when I achieved quite a lot of my success as a bowler. I suppose some of the batsmen didn't know whether to hit me for four or six, so I got them in two minds, and when they didn't hit me for four or six, I probably got them out!

"I'll give you two incidents of my bowling. I'll never forget I was booed off the field at Hove—the one and only time I was booed off the field—the reason being, that I arrived half an hour late, August bank holiday down there, owing to a traffic jam, which nobody believed, but it was. I changed very quickly, and went onto the field, at about quarter to one. Bill Edrich was the captain and after about ten minutes on the field, he said, 'Come and have a bowl!' So I did, at about one o'clock, and by half past one, which was lunchtime, I'd secured three scalps, namely George Cox, Hubert Doggart, and the Reverend—later the Bishop of Liverpool—David Sheppard! Three for practically nothing, and all genuine chinamen and googlies, and I got two LBW and one bowled. As I went off the field I didn't think about anything else, I thought, 'That's marvellous!' and the crowd, in the members, actually said, 'You had no right to bowl there, because you'd only been on the field for about ten minutes when you were put on!' I'd never thought of it that way, but I suppose in a way they were quite right.

"That was one occasion, and the other, I suppose, was probably the greatest disappointment in my life, when Australia made 404 to beat us in the last innings at Headingley in 1948. Norman Yardley put me on to bowl, and I got Lindsay Hassett out, caught and bowled. Then I was put on at the other end after lunch, when the great Sir Donald Bradman came in. I had Don dropped twice before he'd scored 10, genuine googlies which he edged, to dear old Jack Crapp, who was normally a marvellous slip fielder, and he dropped both of them. I would never have forgotten getting the great Don Bradman out in a Test match!'"

He mentioned that first occasion at Hove, when he arrived a little bit late for the start. That was something that was going to stay with him throughout his career. He was noted for not being particularly punctual. "I must say it was one of my great weaknesses. I never realised what time was about. I always left everything 'till the last minute. I hated catching a train and waiting for half an hour, I just wanted to get on to the platform, on to the train, and off we go, but it doesn't always work out that way. No, I was a very unpunctual chap, and I'm not sure whether I've improved a great deal."

Middlesex v. Sussex games on bank holidays were big occasions with full houses at Hove or Lord's. Compton's Middlesex colleague Peter Parfitt used to tell a tale about the gates at Lord's being closed at 10.30 before such a match. "Of course, they had to open them again at 11.30 to let Compo in." Those crowds of nearly 30,000 must have been an excellent grounding for him when he made the transition to Test cricket. "Indeed, yes. I always felt that I was very, very lucky indeed. But my success, if I may call it, in first-class cricket, and the hundreds I made, or the fifties, or the good knocks, and of course the bad ones, were played in front of a lot of people. That used to give me a great deal of inspiration. When I saw all those people out there, I thought, 'Oh my God, I must try and do well here, with them watching!' It stimulated one with big crowds."

Compton warmed to the crowds, and it was not long before the crowds were warming to him in a big way. When was he first aware of that? "I suppose I was aware of it from about 1938, just for the two years, and then the war came, but I was very much aware of it after the war. I used to get a wonderful reception, going in to bat, not only here, and I've always felt very lucky to play most of my matches on this wonderful ground at Lord's, but away from home as well.

"I never forget going to Swansea and playing, in 1947, when I found it very difficult not to get a hundred. I arrived at Swansea, and there were 84 steps to reach the actual playing surface. We went in to bat, and I walked down those 84 steps, and I got the most fantastic reception from the Welsh crowd. And I always remember the bowler at the other end, who was a veteran of 50 then, J.C. Clay, who was a marvellous off-spinner. I said to myself, conceitedly, 'Now, I mustn't take advantage of the old boy.' He's been a great bowler, and I'm going to treat him with the greatest respect. I took guard, first ball he bowled, just outside the off stump, and I sort of rather casually played forward, and it turned, hit the middle stump, first ball. So I was bowled by J.C. Clay for nought in 1947. And I walked off the field to an even greater reception, and it's a long walk up those 84 steps, but it's there in Wisden!"

Going back to before the war, it was only a year after making his Middlesex debut that he was appearing for England. "That's right. 1937, the last Test match against New Zealand, at the Oval, in which Walter Robins, who was then our Middlesex captain, was captain of England. I batted number six then, and that was the beginning of my series of rather disastrous run-outs, although this one was no fault of mine. I was batting with dear old Joe Hardstaff—he was a marvellous cricketer—and I'd reached 65 and I then suddenly thought, 'My gosh, wouldn't it be wonderful to get a hundred in my first Test.' Joe was at the other end, and he was batting against a chap called Vivian, who was a very good New Zealand left-arm bowler. Joe, who was a very graceful batsman indeed, hit the ball back like a rocket, and it touched Vivian's hand onto my wicket, and of course I was backing up, and run out 65.

"That wasn't my fault, but it started me off, and it would never cease, a series of disastrous run-outs, including one against my brother in his benefit match! That was awful. The benefit was, I think, about 1951. Leslie came in, and the dreadful thing was, nobody deserved the benefit more than Leslie, because he'd been marvellous. And I thought, 'Wouldn't it be lovely if the two of us had a good stand.' Anyway, I played a ball down to third man, I was quite set with about 30 or 40 runs, and I said, 'Come one, come two!' because I'd forgotten that George Cox was probably one of the great fielders in those days, and of course Leslie, poor chap, was run out by yards, without ever receiving a ball! I thought, 'Oh, my God, how awful,' and as he passed me, he said, 'I'll forgive you only if you score a hundred for me today.' And fortunately I did, but I proceeded to run out four more in that same innings!

"I was never a great judge of a run, although there were one or two people I could run with. Peter May, always, Godfrey Evans, yes. I think W.J., Bill Edrich and myself, we were slightly dodgy, but it was nearly always my fault. But at least I look back and think, well, most of the run-outs were my fault, but I was quite consistent about it, I used to run myself out just as much as the others!"

Trevor Bailey went on record as saying, "A call from Denis Compton was merely the basis for the opening of negotiations." "And E.W. Swanton once said he used to call his partner for a run, and as he passed him, he said, 'Good luck!'"

The war came fairly early in his career, just three years after he had made his first-class debut. He went to India and played a lot of cricket there, with success. He also played wartime interna-tionals at soccer, so it sounds like he had quite a good war. "I don't think India was that good, but enjoyable. But at the beginning, here, they had this international football, and Arsenal used to play at Tottenham's ground, and the Army used to let me off on a Saturday afternoon, to play in these matches. And of course, there was not much going on in the first part of the war. It was quiet, nobody really thought there was a war on, and so the troops used to flock to see some sport, to liven up their life because it was a pretty grim one.

"Then I went to India, and when I first arrived there, I was greeted by Douglas Jardine, Joe Hardstaff, Peter Cranmer, R.T. Simpson, we all seemed to arrive at Bombay at the same time. Somebody got the idea that we'd have a European side to play

All India while we were there, which we did. Huge crowds came, but we used to get murdered by the Indians, who used to beat us easily.

"I'd gone to Burma, and there, when the war was over, I was coming out of the Army, and the commanding officer said to me that I could do something very good out there before going home, and that was to go and entertain the troops in the jungle, and play against the various companies, which we did. They used to cut trees down in the jungle and make some sort of a football pitch, and it was marvellous because there was nothing for the poor troops out there to do. It was not a very comfortable life in the jungle, but they were stuck there, and so it was fun to give them pleasure. At the end of that, I got a message from my commanding officer to say I was going home in a week's time, but in the meantime there was a match being played in Bombay, and I'd been asked to play in it. It was the Ranji Trophy final. I qualified, because I'd spent about three months in Mao in central India. He said, 'Do you want to play in it?' I said, 'Well, what do you think, sir? He said, 'Well, why not, you're going home in a week's time, why not play in that, and then go straight on to the troopship and go home?'

"So I went down there. I didn't know the Ranji Trophy, or how important it was to them, but I was soon jolly well reminded by a very wealthy Indian merchant, who said to me, 'Mr Compton, we are very, very pleased to have you, honoured to have you in our team. But this is a very important final for us, it's the biggest trophy, it's like your cup finals and Test matches in England, and we would dearly like to win it. So much so, that I will give you a hundred rupees for every run you score over a hundred.' I thought, 'Well, I've got to get a hundred first.' I suppose a hundred rupees was about £7.50 now."

In the first innings he was out for 20, but in the second innings, with Holkar needing 867 to beat Bombay in a timeless match, he hit the jackpot. "I batted with a great Indian called Mushtaq Ali. I got to 100, and then I suddenly remembered what the wealthy merchant had said. I thought, 'Well, every time I hit the ball through the covers for four now, that's 30 quid, nice!' So I eventually got to 249 not out, and number 11 got out, silly old thing. So I worked it all out, and it was about twelve hundred quid, a fortune! I walked off the field, and the captain, who was C.K. Nayudu, a very famous Indian cricketer, came to me and gave me an envelope. I thought, 'My goodness me, I've got the money already! A cheque, that's fine!' So I opened the envelope, and it said, 'Dear Mr Compton, very, very well played indeed, but regrettably I've been called to Calcutta on urgent business.' That was the nearest I got to a fortune. He never paid up."

It was on his return from India that he enjoyed his best-ever season, with 3,816 first-class runs at an average of 90.85, during 1947. "Before that, when I came back in 1946, straight after the war, I had the most disastrous start. I scored something like 15 runs in eight knocks, which was awful. I didn't know how to bat; picking up a bat then was like picking up a stump. Terrible, my confidence had gone, everything. Eventually I came out against Warwickshire here at Lord's. I pushed forward to Eric Hollies, first ball, and it hit the edge of the bat, and the ball rolled back and just touched the off stump, but it didn't knock the bail off. And I thought, this is ridiculous, and the next ball, I just rushed up the wicket and went, whack! I connected, and it went for six into the grandstand balcony. I never looked back after that. I finished up with about 2,400 runs that year.

"When it came to '47, well, I really don't know what to say. First of all, it was the most marvellous summer. The sun never stopped shining, and everything was conducive to cricket that summer. It just happened that if I edged the ball, it went wide of slip, or if I did make a false shot and gave somebody a catch, they dropped it. It's a wonderful feeling, every time I went to bat I knew that I was going to make a lot of runs. Most extraordinary."

And Bill Edrich was usually at the other end. "Indeed he was, yes. Against the South Africans, who were lovely chaps. Alan Melville was the captain, a marvellous cricketer. In fact, he got two hundreds in the Test match in Nottingham. Athol Rowan, Dudley Nourse, who was a legend in South African cricket. It was a great series, really, and tremendous crowds came as well, and that stimulated one. I was never a player to seek records. If it happened, that was very nice. No, I think I got the greatest pleasure in, if I'd scored runs, it was perhaps a match-winning effort for my team. That gave me a lot of pleasure."

The 18 hundreds Compton scored that season eclipsed the record set by someone who he said was his boyhood hero, Jack Hobbs. "At first, I was never conscious about that, when I got eight, nine, ten, and eventually, getting closer to it, of course I was reminded every day by the papers. And so, when I pitched up eventually at Hastings to play for the South of England, again against the South Africans, I needed the one century, I'd got 16, to pass the great Jack Hobbs's record. Obviously I was very conscious of it then, and that was the one time I did seek a record, because everybody reminded me of it. I managed to get the 17th with a great, great friend of mine, Brian Valentine, who captained the Kent side, so that was marvellous."

His 18th century came in the last match of that season at the Oval playing for Middlesex against The Rest. He scored 246 to round the year off, but had he ever wondered whether the runs would dry up during that season? "No, I never thought about that. It was a summer when I was riding very high, and never thought about whether I was going to have a bad run, although I knew at some stage it was going to happen in my career. I think everybody had a bad time at one period or another, but no, not that year.

"I suppose that gave me a tremendous amount of pleasure, but when I look back, the year that gave me the most pleasure was the next year, 1948. Not because I broke any records, although I had a marvellous season, but I had a pretty marvellous series against the Australians, who I considered to be the greatest side that's ever come to this country. I don't know whether that is so, but a great number of people, even now, thought it was. Bradman was captain, you had Barnes, Brown, Miller, Lindwall. Harvey came, a fantastic all-round side, and I suppose that because I succeeded—we lost, of course, 4–1—but having been successful in that series gave me a tremendous amount of pleasure and satisfaction, because I knew that they were a great side, and it's always nice to succeed against very strong opposition, rather than moderate or poor."

A good side to play against as well, because he'd always been great friends with people like Keith Miller. "Absolutely, yes, it was very good. Very hard, I mean, Bradman was a very tough, but brilliant, captain. As you say, Keith Miller and I were the greatest of friends. We're always telephoning each other now, but we were great friends then. But that was off the field. When it came to performing on the field, I was just as likely to get a bouncer first ball from him, round the head, as not, so there was nothing friendly about our competitive spirit on the cricket field. I remember him on one occasion, here at Lord's, he bowled me a bouncer, and he said, 'That's not the only one you're going to get, Compo.'

"No batsman really enjoys playing exceptional speed, and I

must say Miller and Lindwall, they had that. If Miller was in the mood, he could be as quick as anybody. Sometimes, if he'd gone to bed early, he was rather placid, but if he'd had a few drinks, and a bit of a hangover, he could be very quick. And of course there were others. I think probably the fastest bowler that I've ever played against was Frank Tyson. For two seasons, he was phenomenal in speed. And then you had the two South African bowlers, Peter Heine and Neil Adcock, my gosh, they were quick, and that was a wonderful series, 1955, in which we won 3–2. We won by 70 runs in the last Test at the Oval, but that was a tremendous series.

"I didn't like playing against fast bowling, nor does anybody, but you've got to equip yourself against it, and you've got to decide on which is the best technique. I decided at a very early stage that the best way of playing the fast bowler, and the best chance you've got, is to be on your back foot before the ball is bowled, because you can hit a half-volley off the back foot almost as well as you can off the front. It gives you that split second more time in which to either move away, or get in the right position to play them. I used to say to Keith, 'Who were the batsmen you didn't like bowling against, I don't mean so much by talent, but what didn't you like?' He said, 'I never liked a batsman to play on the back foot against me, and I couldn't see the stumps. I like to see the stumps.' And I said, 'Oh, that's very interesting,' and Lindwall was the same. He liked to have a good view of the wicket."

Even with this technique he did occasionally get pinned; there was one famous occasion, at Old Trafford in 1948, when Lindwall got the claret flowing. "Yes, that is quite true, but again, that was nothing to do with my technique. Lindwall bowled me this bouncer, or short one, and I could have played it very comfortably off the back foot, but the umpire called no ball, so I changed my shot and played a hook at the very last second. It hit the top edge, and hit me in the forehead. That's the only time, really, that I've ever been hit. But again, I never forget, I came back with a few stitches and a plaster, and I thought, 'Well, I suppose they'll take it easy,' but not a bit of it. I suppose, for about four overs by both Lindwall and Miller, it was the fastest piece of sustained bowling I'd ever faced in my life, and I was petrified. Fortunately I managed to survive, and of course, that hundred I scored then probably gave me more pleasure than any other hundred I'd ever scored."

As an established and very successful member of the England team, Compton went on a number of overseas tours. However, he would have gone on more had it not been for the fact that his contract with Arsenal gave the football club first call on his services during the winter months. "That's true. I think Arsenal twice refused to let me go on tour. The first was in 1938, to South Africa. I was selected to go there and the Arsenal said, 'No, we want you to rush down the wing for us,' so I didn't go, and Hugh Bartlett went in my place. And immediately after the war, when Gubby took the side to the West Indies, the Arsenal said, 'No, we want you to play football.' So they were the only two tours I didn't go on. I went to South Africa twice, and Australia three times, and the West Indies actually only once, because I could only have gone twice, and once I was turned down."

Despite the disappointment of missing cricket tours, he still enjoyed his footballing career. "I loved the game, I really enjoyed it. If anybody said, did it give you more pleasure, or as much pleasure, as cricket, no. Cricket was a game which didn't end with close of play. There was comradeship and friends, and it's much deeper than football. Football would be an hour and a half, you came off the field and that was the end. You showered, you had a bottle of lemonade, and you left, and that was it."
It is rumoured that he had a little bit more than lemonade to help

him through the 1950 Cup Final for Arsenal against Liverpool.
"I did, I'm afraid. Not by accident either, but I hadn't played very well in the first half, and it was drizzling with rain, and as so many people have said of the hallowed turf at Wembley, I found it very exhausting. I came in at half time, and I felt so tired and one of the greatest legends of all time in football, who played for Arsenal, and he and I were great friends, Alex James, was in the dressing room and I told him this exactly. 'Alex, I'm not playing very well, I'm so exhausted, I'm making no excuses, but it's so tiring out there.' He said, 'Come with me.' So we go to the back of the bathroom, and goodness knows, I thought he was going to give me a lecture, and tell me what to do. Not a bit, he said, 'Take this,' and he gave me the largest brandy! 'I can't, it's a Cup Final! I never drink brandy, never drunk it in my life,' I said. 'Take it,' so I downed this, and I went out in the second half, had a blinder, and didn't feel tired at all!"

Arsenal won 2–0, but did Compton provide any of the goals from the left wing? "I helped with the second goal. Reg Lewis, who I thought was a very great centre forward, scored both goals. But that was a marvellous feeling. I was lucky to play in the Cup Final, really, because I hadn't got into the third round, and I was never really going to be a regular Arsenal first-team player, because of the cricket. But the outside left then, Ian McPherson, God bless him, had two very indifferent games in the third round and the fourth round. Suddenly, the fifth round came along, and we were drawn at home against Burnley, and I saw to my amazement on the team sheet on the Friday morning, I was in the side for the fifth round of the FA Cup.

"I scored a goal, we won two-nothing, and then we played Leeds in the sixth round, we won one-nothing, and then we had this tremendous tussle against Chelsea in the semi-final. Two games, both played at the Spurs ground, and I thought, 'Well, this is marvellous; I think there's a chance now that I'm going to actually play in a Cup Final!' But after 20 minutes of the first match against Chelsea, I said, 'Well that's the end of that, my ambition to play at Wembley,' because Roy Bentley had scored two goals for Chelsea, and they were two-nothing up, and playing magnificently, and we were not in it. Anyway, we got one goal just on the verge of half time. Cox, our right winger, scored direct from a corner, which is quite unusual. There was a bit of a strong wind, and the ball went in. I suppose the goalkeeper had made a mistake. And then, about five or six minutes from time, I took a corner and brother Leslie came up, much to the disgust of Joe Mercer, dear old Joe, who'd said, 'Leslie, stay back, and let's see another one going up, a big tall fellow and very good in the air.' And I crossed the ball, which I think was lucky, to perfection for Leslie, running on, and he headed the equaliser. And in the replay the following Wednesday, we beat Chelsea one-nothing, that's how we got to the final."

After the war, he was allowed to go on tour, to South Africa where he scored the fastest triple century in first-class cricket, at Benoni against North East Transvaal. "I've in fact got the freedom of the city now, at Benoni! Yes, my partner was Reg Simpson, who, God bless him, gave me all the bowling, he said, 'You carry on, please!' And really it was never meant to be. I got 100, and then, you know, I just whacked pretty well all the time. I got nearly 200, made the 200, and then I thought, 'Oh well, I should get out now,' and then kept whacking the ball, and middling it, and so it went on. Eventually I got the 300, and was caught on the boundary, in 181 minutes, which when I think of it now, I think, 'Gosh, that was rather quick!'"

He also went on the 1950/51 tour to Australia, as vice-captain to Freddie Brown, but this did not turn out to be a memorable expedition. "I had a very bad Test series. It was funny; again, that's why it's such a wonderful game. You can never really understand why these things happen, because in the state matches, where you played all the top players, like Miller, Lindwall, whoever, I was averaging about 60 or 70, playing beautifully. Came to the Test matches, I don't know. At the start I was either brilliantly caught or inside-edged onto the wicket; I got out in every conceivable fashion you could think of. And of course what happens then is, suddenly from being in form, you're out of form, your confidence has gone, and I never really regained it in the Test matches there. But that's one of those things, and as I say, it is all part of the game. It's not very nice at the time, because you're playing for your country, but it is the beauty of the game, because it can be a very unpredictable one."

But he got his revenge in fine style, hitting the winning runs that got the Ashes back in 1953 after a long, long period. "Yes, that was lovely. Again, that was a marvellous occasion, because it was the first time I'd ever been on a series-winning side, since I started. Against Australia, having played in '38 against them, '48, '50/51, and then it came to '53, and to win the series then was something new, and something very pleasurable."

And he hit those winning runs with his old mate Bill Edrich at the other end. "Yes, that was lovely. Dear old Bill, yes, I miss the old boy very much indeed. He and I were great friends. Do you know, in all our years of association, we never had a cross word between us? Rather saying something, isn't it? I'll tell you one story. In 1946, in Australia, the players used to have to share rooms. Of course, I always shared with Bill, and we'd come to Sydney, to play the Test match there, and Bill had had a great war record too, he was a pilot in Blenheims, which weren't very safe, they had heavy casualties. But Bill got a DFC, marvellous. Anyway, we get to Sydney, and we're sharing this bedroom. I go to bed about 11

*Compton hits the winning runs as England beat Australia
to win the Ashes at the Oval in 1953*

o'clock the night before the Test, and Bill wasn't there. And I wake up, no Bill! So of course I ruffle his bed, and all that sort of thing, and up comes Wally Hammond, the captain. He said to me—this is at 9.15 in the morning—'The coach is going to leave at 10.30 sharp for the ground.' 'Yes, skipper.' He said, 'Where's Bill?' 'Oh,' I said, 'golly! Surely you know Bill's habits on the morning of a Test match?' 'No, what are they?' I said, 'He gets up and runs around the block, always does that.' 'Oh, does he?' I said, 'Oh, yes,' and he said, 'Well, make sure that you tell him that the coach leaves at 10.30.' 'Very good,' I said, 'that's fine.'

"And of course he pitches up at ten o'clock in the morning, and didn't look very good either, but it's not for the reasons people think. But anyway he got ready, and I said, 'What's happened, where did you go last night?' He said, 'Well, I met one of my flying colleagues, and we were on many, many raids together, and I met him yesterday at the cricket ground where we'd been practicing. And I went to his house, to see his family and all that sort of thing, and I'm afraid we fell by the wayside, we both got the bottle out, and talked about the days of the war, and how lucky we are to be here today, and eventually he said there was no point in me coming back to the hotel, so I stayed the night with him, and his wife and family.' That was the reason. Anyway, I thought, 'Well goodness me, I hope we lose the toss and field.' Of course we didn't, we won the toss, and Cyril Washbrook got out very quickly. Bill had to go in about ten minutes after the start of play, looking dreadful. He'd had no sleep, and the extraordinary thing was, he looked awful for about ten minutes, he couldn't play the ball, he played and missed. Anyway he came together again, and he made 71, followed by 119 in the second innings, and that was the greatest Test innings he ever played in his life!"

Apart from sharing rooms on tour, there were a couple of years when he shared the Middlesex captaincy with Bill Edrich. How did that work? "It didn't work. In actual fact, we were totally different in our attitude towards captaincy in our views. I was a gambler, take a chance, I didn't want to draw, and all that sort of thing. But Bill was rather good, more cautious than that. Bill captained for three matches, then I captained three, so the players never quite knew what to do, they didn't know whether they were coming or going. So really, from that point of view it was very unsuccessful."

But did he enjoy captaincy? "I did quite, yes. But I wanted to make it fun. I wouldn't have thought I'd be terribly good today. Well I don't know, I think the crowd would have liked me as a captain, I would have made sure of a result! If I couldn't win, I thought we might as well lose, we don't want to draw. That was my attitude."

Crowds always did love him, and he had a benefit year which was not only successful from his point of view. Business empires were founded on his 1949 benefit, and he was the first cricketer to employ an agent. "Yes, that's right, but it was not my thought, it was a dear old friend of mine, Reg Hayter. In those days I did have, and in no way am I being conceited, tremendous fan mail. I used to have so many letters, I couldn't cope. I'd no idea what to do, and I couldn't answer them. Old Reg Hayter said, 'For God's sake, Denis, you must get somebody to look after all this for you.' And he produced this chap called Bagenal Harvey, and he turned up saying that he'd be my agent, and do a few things for me. That's when he signed me up for the Brylcreem ads, that was really the only reason I had it. He took all my letters, got them all sorted out, sat me down in an organised way, and in those days I was a very disorganised guy, and got me to answer them, sign the autographs. One thing I would say about myself, I had a lot of children used to follow me then, I always made sure I signed the autographs, couldn't refuse them."

With that attitude to organisation it was perhaps not surprising that when he gave up playing, he did not go into cricket administration; he went into journalism, and into business. Did he ever feel that he wanted to get involved with running the game? "No, I wasn't desperately dedicated to the running of the game, and I don't suppose—I am perhaps now more so than then—I was ever really a committee man. It didn't really appeal to me to come up once a week and sit down, and talk about the affairs that the committees do talk about, the running of the club and all that. No, I rather left that to other people. I had a great love for the game of course, still, and used to come and watch it."

Poster boy: Just one of many advertisements featuring Compton, making him one of the first prominent 'celebrity' endorsers

In 1958 he was awarded the CBE in the New Year Honours list.
"That was a marvellous occasion, but it was very funny. I
arrived at Buckingham Palace, and the Queen gave me the CBE,
and she said, 'Mr Compton, how's your head?' I said, 'Well,
Your Majesty, it's perfectly all right, thank you.' And I wondered
what she was thinking. I supposed she thought I'd had a night
out, celebrating my CBE, but it wasn't that at all. She said, 'I said
that to you because I actually saw, when television was in its
infancy, the occasion when you were hit on the head by Mr
Lindwall at Old Trafford. Have you got a scar?' And I said, 'Yes,
I have a small one there, Your Majesty,' and of course it was
nothing to do with the night before!"

*It was not his head that used to attract the attention during his
career years playing, it was always the much-documented
Compton knee.* "Yes, which I must say is very painful now. I find
it very difficult to play golf, with the same knee, because unfortunately when you get older, you get arthritis, and there's not an
awful lot you can do for that. But yes, it plagued me quite a lot
after the '47 tour. I broke down here and had my kneecap taken
out, and I was able to play one more series. I went to South
Africa, but it was very painful then, and that's the reason I
retired. I thought, 'It's now rather painful, and I'm not enjoying
it, and I'm not giving of my best,' and I was a bit of a perfectionist that way. So I decided I'd better call it a day, in 1957."

*Looking back at his career, everybody remembers the carefree
Denis Compton, going down the pitch, falling over and still
managing to cut a four, swashbuckling shots, and a very carefree
way of life as well, and yet he said he was a perfectionist, and he
wanted to give of his best. Did that mean he was a dedicated
player who practised a lot?* "No, I wouldn't say that I was
renowned for my practice, but it was essential to me to go out
into the nets before I batted, to get the feel of the ball on the bat.

Throughout my career I was very conscious of the responsibilities I had to my team, and although I was all the things that you've said I was, looking carefree and unorthodox and what have you, yes I was, to a certain extent, but I also had the basic principles of how to bat. That was very essential, those you've got to have, to be able to play correctly and to play in the unorthodox way that I did, which apparently gave the crowds and other people the impression that was what I was.

"I had the most marvellous career, and I always feel that I'm extremely lucky, that God had given me the pleasure I had, in both my games of football and cricket. The modern game is very different to when I played. Of course, you're never going to change it, and what I'm referring to is the headgear, how they can play with all this headgear, and visors, and protectors, I don't know. Mind you, the one-day cricket, I get a great deal of pleasure out of that, and I would love to have played that, I think I would have enjoyed that immensely. But the headgear, no. There are more players hit now, because they have their helmets on, and they don't move their heads. And the weight of the bats, three pounds, three pounds six? In my day, Bradman used to be two pounds two ounces, three ounces. I was the same, most players were. I think they haven't got time, the bat is too heavy for them, say, to play the hook shot, the square cut. They're always a bit late on it, they don't play those shots as much now, so I'd love to see them go back to the light bat, remove their headgear, and play with a bit more freedom.

"I'd love to play the modern game. I think there are many things we had which they haven't got today. Our wickets were better when I played, they were much faster and very true, which they're not today, which is also detrimental to the game of cricket. You cannot produce great cricketers on bad wickets. Only good wickets produce good batsmen, great batsmen, good bowlers, great bowlers. Good wickets. You get a very indifferent bowler getting six or seven wickets on a bad wicket. Get him on a good wicket, he can't bowl. No, I think, if we could only get a 50% improvement on our wickets, that would help improve our standards."

And a bit more of the Compton fun in the game? "I think so, yes. I mean, today I notice, after the day's play, in Test matches in particular, you never see the opposition come into your dressing room, or our team going in to the opposition dressing room. Well, we used to play it very hard, but after the game we'd go and have a few beers with the Australians, the South Africans, or New Zealanders or vice versa, they'd come to us. It was much more friendly, and we got a lot of fun out of it, too."
It was a good few years ago that he made his debut at Lord's, and now this same ground is graced by the Compton stand, to say nothing of the Edrich stand as well. That must have meant a lot to him. "When I was asked if I would allow my name to be used for a stand, my reply was, I suppose a very obvious one, to say that would give me great pleasure, and indeed you couldn't have bestowed a greater honour upon me than to have a stand named after me here at Lord's. Yes, that was a wonderful honour for me."

An honour richly deserved, for in the long history of the ground there can have been nobody who exuded more charisma than Denis Compton. That was what endeared him to generations of followers. Both his sons, Richard and Patrick, had limited first-class playing careers with Natal in South Africa, but Richard's son Nick, Denis's grandson, returned to England to complete his education at Harrow before playing for Middlesex, Somerset and England. How much would that have meant to the incomparable Denis Compton?

Doug Insole
born 1926

Doug Insole

SOMEONE WHO HAS BEEN *a vice-captain of England, on tour in South Africa in 1956–57, was twice manager of England touring teams on Ashes tours, chairman of selectors, chairman of what was the Test and County Cricket Board and president of MCC, should know rather more than most about the game. Similarly, someone who made his debut for Essex as long ago as 1947, captained the county throughout the '50s, served two terms as chairman of the club and then became president should know something about Essex cricket in particular. When that man is Doug Insole, both assumptions would be absolutely correct.*

A Cambridge Blue in 1947, 1948, and then 1949 as captain, he played for Essex from 1947 to 1963, and appeared in nine Tests spread over five series between 1950–57. He scored 25,241 first-class runs at an average of 37.61, with 54 hundreds, and passed 1,000 runs in a season 13 times. He took 138 wickets at 33.91, and held 366 catches plus six stumpings. Impressive statistics though these are, all the textbooks describe Doug Insole's attributes with adjectives like "unorthodox", "attacking", "humorous", "rugged", and "resourceful".

That gives the impression that, despite holding the highest offices in the land, he has always regarded cricket as a game to be enjoyed, rather than adopting the attitude of life and death pomposity which regrettably so often goes with positions of power. It is an observation with which he agrees. "Yes, I came into it because I enjoyed it and remain in it because I enjoy it.

When I cease to enjoy it I'll certainly go out of it. When I started with Essex, for example, enjoyment was very much part of the scene because Tom Pearce was running it, but we had to play in a way that was enjoyable because we hadn't got the talent to play in any other way. So it's always been part of my philosophy."

Asked how he first got into cricket, he makes it sound all very straightforward, as if it was a path to be followed by anyone who wanted to make their way to the top of the game. He played for Essex Boys and London Boys before the war, when he was evacuated. When he returned to his home environment after the war he started playing for Chingford and representative sides, and he went into the army where he played a few games before going up to Cambridge. However, it was not as straightforward as it might appear. "It was all a big struggle for me, because I was never orthodox and people didn't think I could bat. Certainly when I started to play representative cricket I used to cut by holding the bat on the slant. I never had any coaching up to that point at all, so somebody taught me in my first Essex trial game how to cut. When I first played for London Boys, for example, I batted at number nine or ten and fielded cover. There were four run-outs on the Surrey side, all down to me, but I still batted down the order. I gradually worked my way up by getting a few runs."

Insole went to the Sir George Monoux School in Walthamstow, but he did not find cricketing inspiration there. Instead, it was his father who was "always very encouraging and very keen. I used to think sometimes a bit too keen, and while he was no great cricketer he was an enormous sports enthusiast."

So was it inevitable that he was going to play for Essex? "Well, I supported Essex from the time I started showing an interest in cricket, which was about four or five. The first Test series I was interested in was the Bodyline series, and I remember listening to reports at 6.15 in the morning, and hearing that rotten signature tune coming over, and wasting half of the quarter of an hour they used to give us. I was born in Middlesex, but only really had any early interest in Essex."

It was when he went up to Cambridge that his career really got on track. "I had some nets early on in the season and was not regarded terribly highly. They stuck me in the second team where I got some runs, and when an opening appeared in the University side, I got in, against Yorkshire. I do remember getting 40-odd before I was given run out—I still don't think I was out—and things didn't seem to go too badly from then on."

"Not too badly" is Insole's modest way of saying that he made a very satisfactory start to his first-class career. After the university campaign he went on to play for Essex and finished the season having played 27 matches, scoring 1,237 runs at an average of 34.36. In addition, he held 24 catches, had three stumpings and three wickets. He recorded a highest score of 161 not out for Cambridge University against Hampshire at Portsmouth, and in that season he also recorded his first century in the County Championship with 109 not out against Lancashire at Clacton.

Maybe Insole was playing at the right time for his style of player. Nowadays it is perhaps more difficult for unorthodox players to progress. "There was more variety and so it was possible to have many more weaknesses, and I certainly had weaknesses. Because I played across the line I was a good player of in-swing bowlers and a good player of off-spinners. But I wasn't anything like as good against away-swingers and leg-spinners and orthodox left-armers, of whom there were plenty, so I had to organise a technique to play those."

Did this unorthodox and very individual technique require good surfaces on which to play? "One would have liked them and we hear a lot nowadays about uneven bounce, but in fact Essex wickets were park wickets and always fizzing all over the place. If you look back at the scores in the '50s and you look at grounds like the Oval, you'll see that people were picking up 6 for 19, and matches were over in a day or two, so obviously one preferred even surfaces, but they weren't always there. In fact, when we had our strongest side in international cricket in the late '50s and you look at the number of hundreds scored in first-class cricket, it was very tiny indeed. We had a very good attack, bowlers were on top and that was why we were winning our matches."

University cricket just after the war was a lot stronger than in later times, when it struggled to maintain first-class status. You only have to look at Insole's contemporaries at Cambridge for the calibre of player to become evident. Which of them stand out in his memory? "Trevor Bailey, obviously. We played in the soccer side in our first term. I didn't know him at all then, but we got to know one another very well. He was the most prominent of those in my first two years, I suppose. John Dewes was there, and he got into the England side. Hubert Doggart was there in my second year, and in my third year when I was skipper we had John Warr, so we had quite a useful side. It was a great season, 1949. We had a very, very congenial cricket side at the university and we enjoyed ourselves immensely. We beat Oxford, who were in fact the only team in England to beat the tourists that year and they beat more or less everybody else, and that's the object of the exercise when you're at university, so all in all it went very well."

When Doug Insole was starting out on his first-class career, it was entirely normal for captains of county sides and, indeed, the England team to be amateurs. Some were barely able to hold a place in their team, but it was thought only right and proper that leadership qualities would be found in those who did not depend on the game for their living. Insole was definitely worthy of his place in the side, and after his success with Cambridge it was a natural progression to get the asterisk next to his name on the scorecard.

Was captaincy something that always appealed to him? "It seemed to be something I got shoved into rather than volunteering for, but it appealed because I was always thinking about the game, and wondering who should be doing what. But I never consciously set out to be captain, any more than I set out to get into cricket administration. I just sort of sidled into it and enjoyed it while I was doing it, but never had any ambition in that way at all. People elected me captain and I accepted with alacrity. Obviously, if you wanted to play the game in a certain way it's a tremendous advantage to be able to say to people, 'That's the way we're going to play, lads.' Not quite 'If you don't like it, lump it,' but 'That's the way I'm going to do it, and if it's not what's required they'll presumably find somebody else.'"

Nowadays there is a significant jump in class between university and county cricket, but back in the 1940s, when undergraduates had normally done their national service before going up, they had more to offer in terms of cricketing maturity. Even so, how did Insole find the transition from university to county? "It was very easy, because the Essex dressing room has always been a very good place, and there was never any acrimony whatsoever about an amateur young whippersnapper coming in. They were all tremendous. It was difficult to take over as captain, because when I did take over it was in the middle of a season and we were at the bottom of the table, where we stayed until the end of that season.

"We then needed to do a considerable bit of pruning, and that was the difficult bit. I had to suggest that two or three of the senior pros were past their best, and that didn't make me the most popular man, for a while anyway. It was also not terribly easy to get some of the older guys, more staid in their ways, to fall in with and enjoy things like fielding practice in the mornings. I was very keen on that, and when we had a younger side we became a very good fielding side, but other than that, from a personal point of view, Essex has always been a great place to play cricket."

Once the pruning had taken place Insole was left with a core of solid professionals who, at the same time as being reliable, offered plenty in the way of diversity and entertainment. "Peter Smith was in the first touring side after the war as a very good leg-spin bowler, but with a very obvious googly. I always used to say that the band used to stand up to play 'God Save the Queen' as it came out of his hand, but on good wickets he was a very big wicket-taker. Ray Smith was a marvellous cavalier cricketer, who bowled inswingers and often had to go round the wicket to contain the swing. He was a tremendous hitter, a very good fielder, a great sportsman and I can't speak too highly of him. He was a lovely bloke to have around.

"Dickie Dodds was one of the great entertainers. He went grey very early and looked old, but was always very lithe and a tremendous striker of the ball, who hit the first ball of the match for six on at least two occasions when I was playing. He was mildly eccentric in some of his ways. I do remember at the Oval, we took a wicket when Ken Preston was bowling from the pavilion end; I was at first slip and Trevor Bailey at second slip. Ken Barrington was next man, and he came in and took guard, and hit the first ball on to his pad and down to fine leg, where we thought Doddsy was fielding. We looked round and there was no sign of Dickie, so we sort of tossed a coin and I went after it to the long boundary; there were no ropes in those days. As I got to within about 20 yards of the concrete wall with the ball slowing down, Dickie Dodds came leaping over the wall, having been to the loo and having taken some little more time than he thought.

"Also at the Oval I recall my worst piece of captaincy ever. Geoff Whittaker, who was an enormous hitter, skied Peter Smith and Dick Horsfall was fielding at long-on and Dickie Dodds was at long-off. I called 'Dick' and the two met right in front of the pavilion gates, collided head on and the ball fell between them. I always called surnames after that, even though we had three Smiths in the side at one time.

"Dickie Dodds was also one of the first batsmen to wear a helmet, in a sense, in that he put the inside of a baseball hat into his cap, because he was occasionally getting hit on the nut. It caused a bit of surprise, especially to one F.S. Trueman, who hit him on the head before the ball went to the boundary. In the mid-50s he was a compulsive hooker. He used to hook half-volleys almost, but he was a tremendous entertainer."

Entertainment was the key word for Essex at the time. With Dickie Dodds opening and Insole himself to come in a little later, it was never going to be dull watching the county. "We couldn't afford for it not to be, because we didn't have a good enough side technically to hope to win very much. The *News Chronicle* did start an entertaining batting competition, and we won it three years running and they abandoned it. Dick Horsfall was a good striker of the ball, as were the two Smiths. We got the fastest hundred of the season, I think, seven years out of nine. Even an amateur called Colin Griffiths came in and got the fastest hundred of the season at Tunbridge Wells one year.

"Our main weakness was that we never had a finger spinner who was really any good until the late '50s, and finger spinners were essential. Yorkshire and Surrey, the two major sides, were absolutely stacked with them and very good ones at that. Trevor was the mainstay of our bowling right the way through, and of course he was playing quite a few Test matches. England immediately after the war hadn't got a fast bowler at all. John Warr was sent to Australia as a fast bowler, Brian Statham went as a replacement and he was the first sign of the new wave. But Ken Preston was a really quick bowler in 1948–49, who broke his leg playing football. It didn't really mend properly, so he couldn't run in and bang his leg down. So he changed his method entirely over a couple of years, when he went into the second XI and started bowling cutters and swingers, and he became a very fine bowler; he was a tremendous professional.

"In the early days Peter and Ray Smith bowled thousands of overs; 3,000 overs between them more seasons than not. Both were very good bowlers, but not necessarily match-winning bowlers, so we were really short of that category. Roy Ralph came in a bit later on. He was a very useful swing bowler from club cricket, who was better in first-class cricket than club cricket because he tended to have his catches held. He came into the side at 33, and I think paid Essex cricket a great compliment, because he came to me at the end of the first season in which he'd played a fair bit of cricket, and asked if I thought the club would play him as professional the following season, because he was playing as an amateur. He said he might as well have the money, because there was no particular advantage to being an amateur in that side, which was an indication to me that they all felt they were getting a fair crack of the whip.

"We did tend to play a lot of amateurs and, like Trevor, I wanted to make sure that nobody felt they were coming in just for the sake of coming in. We were always anxious to play the best side, and if we thought an amateur was better than the pro, we put them in. But it was essential that they were there on equal terms with the pros, and that's what they all accepted."

Throughout any conversation with Doug Insole, the name of Trevor Bailey crops up time and time again. After meeting at Cambridge University, their careers appeared inseparable. The Essex records were studded with partnerships between them, and Insole himself would concede that Bailey was the more talented player, but just how good was he? "He was a very fine all-rounder and would rank with the best of our all-rounders since the war. His bowling was controlled, and was dangerous when he got any help from the wicket. He was always a great spotter of batsmen's weaknesses and strengths, which was one of his great virtues to me as a captain. He wasn't necessarily the greatest reader of a game, but in terms of the detail of it he was very good indeed.

"As a batsman, he had a very good technique but he tended to be a one-paced player, and there were numerous occasions when that was absolutely invaluable for Essex, because he was getting runs in the middle of the order while everyone else was getting out. He was quite capable of banging the ball around, but it seemed to take a big change in his mental attitude; a bit like Geoff Boycott. He tended to get into a frame of mind that they shall not pass, and it's very difficult to alter it. I used to tell him when it was expected of him to go in and thrash it around, but he never really enjoyed that, but he'd always do it because he was a very good team man. He used to moan afterwards if he got out, but we did once both score a hundred before lunch, possibly that's the only time it's been done. It was a match against Nottinghamshire in the 1950s. He had the strokes but they just had to be brought out of him. He was a very useful fielder, excellent in the slips. He was never a great thrower but had a very safe pair of hands. He had small hands, which made it not very easy for him to catch skiers, but he was a very good instinctive slip fielder. They were brittle hands too, which bust with great regularity.

"I had one major upset with him that I can remember, and that was in 1953 when he was playing in the Leeds Test and we were at the bottom of the table. He rang from Leeds and said he was extremely tired and thought he could do with three days off. His wife Greta was up there, so he thought they'd sort of mosey down and he'd play on the Saturday. I wasn't in favour of that at all and I said so. I'd either just got out or was about to go in, and so was feeling a bit tetchy anyway, so I said it was just not on and he could either appear in the morning or forget the rest of the season. Whether it would have ever come to that I don't know, but it was something I said on the spur of the moment. Anyway, in the morning there he was, and it was a bit tense. We didn't say too much to one another for a couple of days, but he got 70-odd not out in our innings against Somerset and then took four for 30 in their first innings to make them follow on. In the second innings a lad called John Baker came in at number eight. Trevor bowled him out for nought a second time. Having done that, well into the second day, he came over to me and said that if he'd been told Baker was playing there would have been no argument. That was that, it was all forgotten and away we went. In fact we won six of the next eight games, which got us seven or eight places up the table, which for us was quite a feat.

"When I was captain it was very much a team effort between us. I don't think there was any doubt, in my mind or his, who was to have the last word, but we consulted a hell of a lot. We shared rooms the whole time, we had a lot of common interests and we were very close. It was a magnificent ten or 12 years. It was, in the end, very unfortunate that he, as I think he later admitted, went on a bit too long. It was a great shame, because after all he had done people shouldn't have been able to say that it was time he gave it away. In the end, I was the guy who had to say that we didn't need him the following season, which was a great sorrow to me and ruptured things for a time, but we continued to be great friends."

As mentioned, Doug Insole took over the Essex captaincy from Tom Pearce in 1950 when the county was at the foot of the table. He went about getting a side together that usually managed to finish in the top half of the Championship for the next decade, without ever actually challenging for honours. "We needed to have some changes, because there were some guys who really weren't good enough by then. One of those was Tom Wade, who'd been a tremendous wicket-keeper, and it was sad to have to say that we needed another 'keeper. In the event we got hold of Paul Gibb, and that was a tremendous coup because he did us six or seven years of magnificent service.

"He was a very stubborn man, extremely obstinate, but on the other hand extremely pleasant. He was an enormous eater, and was the sort of man who would break down in the Blackwall Tunnel or get a puncture on a Saturday morning, and he'd calmly get his tool kit out and start mending it, taking 35 minutes or so with people threatening to beat him up because of the congestion he was causing, but he was completely unperturbed. Nobody wanted to travel with him in his van to away fixtures because he did 28 mph on average, and if we were going to Swansea you'd get there about four in the morning.

"Others I brought in were mainly younger players. We had an established opening pair in Avery and Dodds. Dick Horsfall came in and played regularly, Paul Gibb was at four, I was at five, Trevor at six, but we generally tried to become a little more athletic, energetic and virile. The trouble with having long-serving members of the staff who weren't quite up to it is that they tend to go on playing and block other people, and it's awfully difficult to hoick them out."

The Essex side of the 1950s might have been ideal for one-day cricket, and had the limited-overs competitions been around then, they might not have had to wait until 1979, or 103 years after their formation, to win their first trophy. Insole believes that the batting in the '50s would have been ideal, but the bowling might have proved a little untidy to be effective. He is convinced they would have enjoyed some high-scoring matches, and he even played one limited-overs game himself. "It was in 1969 when I had just finished being a selector, and I'd played a season of club cricket, getting a few runs. We only had 12 professionals at that time, Keith Fletcher was playing for England, somebody else was injured and so Brian Taylor asked if I would play. It was at Yeovil, against Somerset, and I set out about seven o'clock on a Sunday morning and caught the eight o'clock train, which was full of sailors from the Royal Tournament who were desperately hung over. I didn't get a seat. I couldn't get a taxi, so dragged my bag to the ground, and did my fielding practice.

"I wasn't the greatest batsman in the world but I could play off-spinners, and was down to bat at six. Brian Langford bowled 8-8-0-0, the only time it's ever been done, and I was sitting there to go in and hopefully belt him all around the ground. By the time he was off, other bowlers were on and I said to Brian Taylor that there was no point in me going in now, because he needed someone who could cart it all around. He said, 'No, old son. You go in.'

"When I did get in, Greg Chappell was bowling, and I was desperate to give the strike to Keith Boyce at the other end. I played a couple of balls, played a third to square leg and called Boycie through for a single. He sent me back, Langford hit one stump and I was run out for nought.

"We lost the match, and I came home on a train full of people coming back from the seaside. I put my bag down in the corridor and a woman said, 'My son's very tired; could he sit on your bag?' I said yes, but he weed all over it. I got home about midnight or one o'clock. It was a great day and I still haven't had my expenses!"

Not surprisingly, he resisted all entreaties to make another appearance. But as captain of Essex in the '50s, he set about introducing new players to the side. One of them was a Yorkshireman called Gordon Barker, who was in the Army at the time. "He was with us for some time, and then went to Felsted where he produced some very fine cricketers, like Derek Pringle, John Stephenson and Nick Knight. We had every reason to be grateful to him."

It was always a characteristic of Essex cricket that players continued to be involved after their playing days were over, and the public schools in the county were full of former Essex cricketers who took up coaching posts. Insole believed that this was important. "We believed that you need the playing fraternity with their roots in the county to keep the club going. Of course, you need the commercial side and the business side, but although cricket is a business, the business is cricket."

While the objective was always to produce their own players, there were times when they had to look outside for replacements. This helped Essex to climb to the top echelons of the table by beating the leading sides of the time, like Yorkshire and Surrey. But they were equally likely to lose to lowly teams, with

*Insole, as Essex captain, takes runs off the Surrey attack
at the Oval, 1951*

*a glorious unpredictability that was so much a part of Essex
cricket's appeal.* "It certainly appealed to me when I was young,
and I still vividly remember the day we bowled Yorkshire out for
31. I remember cycling along the road shouting to a bloke,
'We've bowled them out for 31,' and I was only about seven or
eight at the time. It was one of those joyous occasions."

Were the seeds of later success evident while he was still playing?
"The answer to that, really, is no. One always hoped for it, but
we needed certain types of players, and until they came through
we were never going to be successful. I always thought that our
attitude was right and good, and without being pious about it
we thought that it was a game for spectators as well as us; if we
didn't enjoy it, they wouldn't. But we weren't in a position to
slaughter teams, so if people were going to watch us, it was
because we entertained them rather than to see us slay the
opposition. People watch winning sides, but they came to watch
us because they thought we were more entertaining than some
who were regularly winning matches.

"Over the years, Essex supporters have been enormously loyal, and even when we were playing badly they stood by us pretty well. There's great enthusiasm in the county, from East Ham through to Frinton, and that's good. It's a sprawling county from the east end of London through to the slightly toffee-nosed areas, but there's great unity which I've always appreciated."

Despite the homely feel that permeated Essex cricket, and the closeness between the members and the players, it would have been only natural for a player of Insole's qualities to perhaps look slightly enviously at counties that were consistently gathering silverware. However, Insole refutes that he ever turned his attention elsewhere.

"I can honestly say that I didn't. It was often said that it was a better achievement to get Essex half way up the table than it was for Surrey to win it. I mean, if Surrey hadn't won it with the players they had, it would have been a sad reflection on them. If we got half way up we hadn't exactly fulfilled our ambitions, because we were always ambitious, and there was one season when we were at the top of the table until the middle of June. Then it was all systems go. Then we had our usual unpredictable five weeks, without getting a single point, and suddenly we were half way down the table again.

"I've always enjoyed tremendously the atmosphere in Essex, which allowed captains then, and still does, to get on with it. I did find, to my surprise, that I was landed with all sorts of jobs, like paying the players, organising transport and paying hotel bills. I didn't mind doing so, but I was surprised that it wasn't being done by some administrative guy behind the scenes. We probably couldn't afford that sort of guy, and we got to the point in the mid-60s when we were pretty well bankrupt.

"There was one year in particular that caused a real crisis, when we lost £9,000 on a turnover of £43,000. Two years after that, when we cut our staff down to 12, we ran it on £33,000 a year. The whole bang shoot—players' salaries, secretary's salary, the lot. But looked at in today's terms when we're turning over a million, that's the equivalent of losing £200,000. We were in a very bad way, so we were obliged to take stringent measures in about 1966. That's when we cut our staff to 12."

With Brian Taylor as captain and the experience of Gordon Barker still there, the rest were young players who showed promise, but who were virtually unknown at the time. "The extraordinarily lucky thing about it was that of those 12 players, six of them became very, very competent players. The likes of John Lever, Robin Hobbs, Ray East, David Acfield, Stuart Turner, and Keith Fletcher. They were fit, they played every game, and they all became very good cricketers; that's partly good judgement, but mostly it's luck.

"Tonker [Brian Taylor] was the chap to lead them, because they needed a certain amount of discipline and he was certainly a disciplinarian. He wouldn't claim to be the greatest tactician ever, but his heart was absolutely in the right place and if you talk to these guys today, they'll tell you what a tremendous man he was for them. We were helped by the one-day competitions coming in, because we were a good one-day side. Trevor brought over Keith Boyce and he was a fabulous cricketer for Essex, a tremendous entertainer but a very, very fine cricketer. We had a great fielding side, some useful bowlers and some explosive batting, and in one-dayers we began to have some influence, although until 1979 we didn't actually win anything.

"I was a bit keener on fielding and a bit more of a disciplinarian than Tom Pearce. When I first got into the side, Tom was getting on. But enjoying your cricket was very much Tom's philosophy. We've always said to the guys at the start of the season that nobody is ever going to criticise you if you lose trying to win, and nobody is going to criticise you if you're trying, but if you've got to employ gamesmanship or lose, then lose."

After Brian Taylor retired, Keith Fletcher took over the Essex captaincy. "He was quite reserved and shy in his early days, and he used to whisper in Tonker's ear. It wasn't until he'd been skipper for two or three years that he started exerting his authority. He always had a very technical appreciation, and he emerged as a tremendous captain and deserved much better things internationally."

On the question of international cricket, Doug Insole played for England in nine Tests spread over five different series. That is hardly a recipe to build confidence and give the feeling of being established in the side. "I don't want to be unduly modest, but I always thought I was quite fortunate to be picked. There was one year when I was getting loads of runs when I thought I was quite unfortunate to be dropped. I thought it was stupid to drop me, to be honest, having got 55 against South Africa.

"In my first match in 1950 I created a change in the law. I was dismissed by Sonny Ramadhin in the first innings. The ball spun back to hit my pads, there was a big appeal for LBW, and then went on to the wicket and out I went. As I turned round Frank Chester was going over to the scoreboard saying, 'That was out LBW not bowled, because the appeal was for LBW and I gave it before the ball hit the stumps.' That was pretty lightening reflexes, so the law was changed to say that if it hit the stumps you were out bowled, whether it had hit your pads, box or anything else.

"Ramadhin was immense as far as I was concerned. I played twice against the West Indies, and I think my top score was 21, and I got two noughts, including the one that enabled Peter May and Colin Cowdrey to put on 411 at Birmingham in 1957."

Insole went to South Africa in 1956–57, as vice-captain to Peter May. It was the only overseas tour he went on with England, despite having been invited to captain them on their tour to India in 1951–52. He was working for George Wimpey at the time, and it was suggested his career would be better served by remaining at home during the winter. With a young family to support, he took the advice. Five years later, his employer gave him permission to tour and he went.

"MCC, who were at that time responsible for selection, were for some reason keen that I should go as vice-captain. It was a very happy tour, very good fun. A good side, we only drew in the end 2–2, but it was thoroughly enjoyable and I had a good tour. I finished top of the averages, played in all the Tests and got my only Test hundred. It was a bit painstaking in a backs-to-the-wall performance, but I was quite pleased with what happened there. I came back as an established member of the side, but started off in '57 playing desperately badly. One of the problems I always had was because I was working, I never practiced. I couldn't take a month off to practise, and so the first match I went into was almost my first net. I started off very badly, and I remember 'phoning Gubby Allen and saying, 'If you're thinking of picking me, please don't, because I'm in no sort of nick.' But they did, and that was the Edgbaston Test. I was driving Freddie Trueman from Droitwich to the ground and he said, 'We'll get millions today, old lad, we'll get millions.' I thought to myself that a million is one and six noughts, and I certainly got one of those noughts! He was trying to bolster my confidence, unsuccessfully."

At the end of the 1963 season Doug Insole decided to retire from first-class cricket, after his employers had suggested that, at the age of 34, they needed more of his time. He was not unhappy at giving up playing, because he was missing quite a few matches through selection duties, and he found batting was getting no easier. That did not mean he was lost to the game, because as well as his business commitments he found time to continue as a selector, and has been involved in administration ever since. "I became a selector in, I think, 1959, nominated by Surrey. Perhaps I was getting too many runs against them and they thought I should miss a few games! It was enjoyable, by and large, even if it wasn't an easy job, but I had a very good lot of fellow selectors. Gubby Allen was chairman, Wilf Wooller and in my first year, Herbert Sutcliffe, and subsequently Willie Watson and Alec Bedser. Walter Robins became chairman in 1961, and he was a good friend and a tremendous performer."

Those selection committees appear to be manned by some strong characters in the game. "Yes, Gubby was completely in charge, but Wilf Wooller was a man of all sorts of ideas, some of them good, some of them horrendous. You could always ignore the horrendous and go for the good. Alec Bedser was a very fine judge, not wildly enthusiastic, but he was a very good judge of a cricketer. Willie Watson was a delightful bloke and also a very good judge, and then we had Don Kenyon, Peter May. I became chairman in 1965, I think. It was the custom then, and probably a good custom, to go from one Australian series to another. That was crucial from an English point of view, so you had the build-up to an Australian series and then you gave it away. Certainly Robbie was a very strong character. Eccentric, he said on a couple of occasions, 'Well, that's long enough. We've been three hours so I'm going to the pictures,' leaving me to sort out the last couple of places or what have you. But he'd made his views pretty well known so we knew what he wanted. He was an advocate of lively cricket. Not ridiculously profligate cricket, but lively cricket."

Undoubtedly the most controversial decision the selection committees Doug Insole chaired had to make was the omission of Basil D'Oliveira from the tour to South Africa in 1968. D'Oliveira had been prevented from playing even first-class cricket in his native land, because the apartheid system prevented Cape Coloured players like him from reaching the upper echelons of the game. He had come to England in 1960 at the age of 29, thanks to the intervention of renowned and respected commentator John Arlott, and appeared in the Central Lancashire League for Middleton while qualifying for Worcestershire. His first-class debut came in 1964, and by 1966 he was playing for England.

He was selected for the first Test against Australia in 1968, making nine and 87 not out. He then went into a dreadful run of form that saw him reach double figures in only one of his next seven innings, and lost his place in the Test side to Colin Milburn. D'Oliveira's lack of form continued, so that between the first and fifth Tests he scored a mere 389 runs for Worcestershire at an average of 18.52. It was therefore something of a surprise when he was recalled for the Oval Test, following the withdrawal of Roger Prideaux. Nevertheless, after being dropped on 31, D'Oliveira went on to make 158, and it appeared his place on the tour to South Africa was a formality. It was not, and when his name did not appear on the list of tourists it caused an understandable outcry.

Insole remembered the build-up to the announcement during another interview in 2013. "Advice was being received from all and sundry almost every day. Newspaper people, broadcasters, the public, until in the end I said in the meeting, 'Look, let's pick a team to go to Australia. Very similar wickets, and we don't have to worry about the other problem,' which is what we did. It still buzzes along now in that certainly, two or three times a year, someone comes on and says, 'What about it?' Somebody wrote to me a couple of months ago saying, 'Now that Basil D'Oliveira's dead, isn't it about time we heard the truth about the selection meeting?' I simply replied that I'd been talking about it for the last 40 years or however long it is, but if you think there's anything of an X factor to reveal, there isn't, so forget it. But that was a difficult decision."

At the time, he had said that in overseas conditions D'Oliveira was not considered to be an all-rounder, and he had to be judged alongside other available batsmen. Colin Cowdrey was England captain at the time and had a say in selection, and is reported to have told D'Oliveira that he wanted him in the side. Don Kenyon, his county captain at Worcestershire, was also on the committee, so he had plenty of representation.

Basil D'Oliveira

Responding to the Cowdrey claim, Insole said: "That's the big mystery, because Colin certainly didn't recommend Basil. In fact, he and Les Ames were the management for the previous tour to the West Indies, and if they had said, 'We want Basil D'Oliveira,' then without very much doubt at all he would have gone. But neither was enthusiastic, and both were happy with the side that was selected."

The man selected in his place was Warwickshire's Tom Cartwright. He suffered a shoulder injury during the latter stages of the season, so did the selectors have assurances that he was going to be fit for the tour? "We had indications, yes. The physio said he thought he'd be OK. Tom was a fine bowler, the best medium-pacer in this country and probably anywhere, and he'd have been terrific in South Africa. But I went up to see him at Edgbaston, and he said that he couldn't be sure that he'd be able to go through the tour, and that was that. He virtually withdrew."

It was thought that Cartwright had secured his place when he appeared for Warwickshire in a one-day game against a Gillette Invitation XI, and bowled his allocation of overs. But there is a world of difference between bowling ten overs in what was little more than an exhibition match and completing an arduous tour. So when he withdrew, the selectors were faced with finding a replacement. "Barry Knight was barred by MCC from being selected, Ray Illingworth wasn't available, nor was Ted Dexter, nor was Bob Barber, nor was Ken Higgs; I remember those names very well. Basil had been getting wickets for Worcester and was top of their bowling averages [he took 61 wickets at 16.22 that season] but hadn't scored a run until the Oval. He was on the reserve list and he just slotted in when Tom dropped out."

Not surprisingly, the reaction was vociferous, with conspiracy theories abounding. Did this disappoint Insole? "I don't think so. There were a number of the top press guys who approved of it; one or two took a sort of righteous view, which is fine. I got hundreds of letters and 'phone calls. 'We thoroughly applaud your decision, signed Adolf Hitler.' That sort of thing; it wasn't a pleasant time."

He gave up his position as chairman of selectors later that year, but was reaction to the D'Oliveira affair an instrumental factor in reaching that decision? "No. It was end of the Australian tour, and I'd already made it clear that I was giving up in May of that year. Most of the time it was very good. It was interesting, it was intellectually testing and it was excellent. We did have the Geoffrey Boycott instance when he was dropped after he scored 240, which he still goes on about, but that was nothing like the same category as the D'Oliveira one. There was a bit of backlash then, mainly from Yorkshire, but otherwise it was very enjoyable."

There was a precedent for Boycott being dropped, because Ken Barrington was once left out after he had scored a particularly slow hundred. "Yes. We did say at the start that we wanted to get things moving more. Ken's was a terrible knock really, a grinding, painstaking knock, and he knew it. But he got a hundred after six and a half hours or whatever and hit the next ball for six. It just illustrated what the prospects might have been. As in the Geoffrey Boycott case, it was a question of losing time. If you're on a really good wicket and you've only got 240 at the end of the first day, even if it's only for four, you're well behind schedule.

"The Boycott Test we only won by a couple of hours on the final day, but he still rants on about it, and understandably in a way. It's not a very common occurrence to get dropped after you get 246. People tend to blame the chairman of selectors, or praise him, but you had four selectors and they were all pretty strong characters. You're not dealing with people who are always going to say 'yes chairman, yes chairman'. They state their minds, and I don't think in my time as a selector we had a vote. It always came about by consensus. It was easy to see from the deliberations the way people were thinking.

"It's all very interesting too, that you get vested interests but not necessarily selfish interests, but county captains were often very loathe to put forward their players. 'He's too young and needs another couple of seasons.' In the case of Colin Cowdrey, he thought that both Derek Underwood and Alan Knott were too young when we picked them. But people playing against them and watching see things differently. Ted Dexter, on the other hand, was mad keen about John Snow and he was dead right. We accepted his view, which was backed up by statistics to an extent, but those outside views were expressed and did come into it. I'm not saying it was wrong, but looking at his temperament and his attitude to situations in the game, either distance lends enchantment to the view, or familiarity breeds contempt. You take your pick."

Doug Insole managed to combine his selection duties with his playing career, and went into cricket administration when he retired, making time for that interest while pursuing his business career. It represented quite a juggling act. "It became very, very difficult. Realistically, I spent the best part of a day a week on cricket administration, either as chairman of cricket or with Essex. My employers were aware of that, and they were prepared to stand it. I changed jobs in 1975, and my new employers asked how much time cricket took up. I said between half a day and a day of their time, and that was accepted. But then I was invited to become chairman of the board, and shortly after that Packer arrived on the scene, involving an enormous amount of time with five weeks in court, and I just had to give it away.

"It had become more and more difficult for people with other work to do it, and I advocated when I left office that we needed, if not a full-time then a non-executive chairman, who was paid to do the job and was available when required. You never know what is going to crop up, because you can sail along with a series of meetings, and then all of a sudden a crisis arrives out of the blue, which is very time consuming. Then you're in it more or less full time with interviews, talking to high commissioners and politicians and so on. So I said that we needed someone whose job it is, even if it's not a full-time job. It's not a job I'd like. Even in the unlikely event I was invited to do it, I've done my whack and am more than happy to bow out. I enjoyed my involvement but I think they need someone coming through to take over. I'm always very interested, and will be around for as long as people want me, but I've got no ambition at all as far as cricket administration is concerned."

He talks continually about being pushed into the captaincy and being asked to do various jobs in the game. Was there anything that he set his mind on doing and went out to get, rather than being asked to do it? "I was quite keen to manage a side or two overseas before I packed up, because it's a tremendous experience, and if you haven't gone through a full tour with a side overseas, you've missed out on a big part of cricketing life, so that I was keen to do.

"The first time I did it was reasonably appropriate, in that it was during the Packer era and I'd been involved with that all through. We were anxious to hold our people together, and in fact we only lost five of our players while other countries virtually lost the lot, so that was a sort of rearguard action out in Australia. But it was also tremendous fun, with a very good lot of blokes, and I enjoyed it immensely, although it was the hardest work I've done. That was something I wanted to do, and

I wanted to be involved with Essex. I'm not saying I didn't want to do the other things, I'm saying that I was never obviously or ambitiously sticking myself forward, and I'd have been quite happy not to."

He mentioned that managing his two tours to Australia was the hardest work he had ever done, but what made it so hard? "You do as much as a tour manager as you think you ought to, and as far as I and most others who've done it are concerned, it's a 24-hour-a-day job. People back home don't seem to realise there's a time difference. You're up early in the morning doing interviews, and then people are knocking on your door at half past one in the morning, pouring out their troubles to you.

"On the second tour in particular, there was a hell of a lot of press and social involvement. Ian Botham was around, and there were a lot of journalists who weren't interested in the cricket who were looking for things, and I spent a lot of time keeping the blokes out of trouble, as it were. That was much harder work because we were losing then, and it's always harder when you're losing because people are looking at you much more critically.

"I remember saying to our blokes when we were two-nil down going to the Melbourne Test, the fourth one. There's a big lounge in the Hilton Hotel and I said, 'You'll be out of that lounge by ten o'clock. If you want to do anything else it's up to you, but get out of there because everyone's in there, and they'll be saying that you're staying up late and drinking and so on. Some asked, 'What's the form if we don't drink?' I said, 'If you're drinking tonic they'll say it was gin and tonic, if you're on tomato juice they'll say it's a Bloody Mary, so get out and don't give people the chance.'

"I remember one of our players was very upset that he'd been criticised by a couple of journalists for getting out for a low score through a 'rash irresponsible stroke', when all he'd done was play forward and get an outside edge. I was talking to a senior member of the press gang about that, and saying how upset he was. He asked if I knew why, and he said it was because he hadn't said hello to anyone in the lift that morning. I asked if he was serious, and he replied that it was human nature.

"If you're involved as a selector or manager it's amazing how you live every ball, and the minute that responsibility goes off, you're just an interested spectator again. You don't have that feeling gnawing away when you bat, bowl and field for them all, and it's a very involved job."

From a modern perspective, it is difficult to understand the marked divide in the game that existed between amateurs and professionals until 1962, when the distinction was removed. In less egalitarian times, the amateurs in some teams would stay in different, usually superior, hotels for away matches, have different changing and dining rooms, and would enter the field through different gates on some grounds. On one celebrated occasion at Lord's, the public address system crackled into life with an urgent-sounding announcement that there was a change to the scorecard. Was it a change that would disappoint the spectators? Was Compton or Edrich not playing? No, the announcement went on: "Instead of F.J. Titmus in the Middlesex side, it should be Titmus, F.J." To differentiate between amateurs and professionals on the scorecard, amateurs had their initials before their surname and professionals afterwards. Doug Insole played an influential part in getting the distinction abolished, having suffered as an amateur himself. "Looking back, it seems ridiculous that I was an amateur. I had a young family and wasn't earning a great deal of money. I wasn't poor, but I was earning nothing from cricket while other guys were getting more from the game than I was earning at Wimpey's. It rankled a bit at the time when I thought, 'These chaps are out here doing the same as me, and earning more than I'm getting for 12 months' work.' It does seem ridiculous that one should have ploughed away playing for nothing. It's all right if you've got loads of money, but I hadn't. In my situation I was unable to do anything else, because I had an employer who wanted me at his beck and call if he wanted me, and you couldn't be under contract to two people."

Insole was on the committee that eventually oversaw the abolition of the amateur/professional divide. That divide was not as wide as it appeared, because there were several so-called amateurs who took a post as assistant secretary with a county in order to take a salary from the game. But he laments one aspect of the loss of amateur status. "I think the game's lost a lot by the loss of the amateur. There was a degree of independence. In my own case I was very keen to play for Essex, but if they didn't like what I was doing I could say, forget it, and go to play for Middlesex or not play for anybody, so one was able to have some sort of influence in that way. In Essex, certainly, the captains did have influence, because they've been the right sort of personalities, and because people felt that was the way they wanted it to go, and if they don't perform we can always take it off them. There's a great deal of handcuffing around the place where people feel they're playing for their places and for their jobs, which wasn't there with an amateur."

After all that went on, it is perhaps not easy to put the names Insole and Packer together in changing the lot of cricketers around the world. But when the Australian came into cricket distributing largesse, Insole was instrumental in raising money to improve the terms offered to English players.

"When I was chairman of TCCB, we got the Cornhill sponsorship for Test matches and that was extraordinary, in that it was done by a ring around to all the county chairmen for their approval of the Cornhill proposal. The only way we could get players' money up was to get a sponsor, so three or four of us did that, with Cornhill wanting a decision very quickly before the end of the season so they could publicise it. But the whole subject of commercialism in cricket is a very interesting one and it's a question of holding a balance, making the game viable but making it enough of a game that people want to be associated with it.

"Funnily enough, when I started, Essex were the only side to have sponsored lunches, and the captain had to go and sit with the day's sponsor at lunch and make polite conversation for 40 minutes, and wait for the bell to go and then dash off. We were actually in the forefront of that on all our festival grounds, when we had no ground of our own. We didn't buy Chelmsford until the late '60s, so played on eight different grounds, one of which, Westcliff, didn't have a toilet, so we had to go out of the ground through the old wooden fence, literally to spend a penny. Since then the whole thing has become much more commercial. As recently as 20 years ago our total budget was £33,000, and it's now well over a million."

For a man who has achieved so much positive in the game, does he have any regrets? "Well, if you've got about three hours... Maybe mostly personal regrets, about not having done better here or there. Those sorts of things, rather than things that have gone cataclysmically wrong. I've regretted having to do a number of things, but I haven't necessarily felt that it was wrong to do them, and in many cases I was required to do them anyway. It was very, very difficult to reduce the Essex staff from 24 to 12; that was horrible. To have a guy like Frank Rist, who's an absolutely marvellous bloke, who eventually worked for us for pretty well nothing. To have to say to him, 'Sorry Frank, but we just haven't got any money so we can't have a coach. If you're prepared to do it we'll pay your expenses and so forth, but that's the best we can do.' And he did that for a couple of years. And I regret obvious things like having to drop Ken Barrington for scoring a slow hundred and having to tell him. A lovely bloke and we were great friends, and we remained great friends. That's not easy. And similarly, Geoffrey Boycott. As chairman of the selectors you become involved with your players, inevitably, and if you do something that is obviously going to hurt them it's something you regret having to do, but you don't necessarily feel it's wrong to do it. It has to be done."

Apart from one or two exceptions, Doug Insole did not go out to seek positions in cricket. He was asked to fulfil certain roles, because his various qualities made him the stand-out candidate. As time went on, and he gained intimate experience of so much that makes the game work, so those qualities became even more indispensable than ever. It had been suggested that he might become president of the MCC on more than one occasion, but it was not until 2006 that he eventually accepted the honour. Cricket and cricketers can be grateful that he undertook so many roles in the game, and performed them to the best of his considerable abilities.

Epilogue

HAVING TRANSCRIBED THESE INTERVIEWS, the thrill of meeting these great cricketers is undiminished. In fact, it is enhanced and at the same time tinged with a touch of sadness because, with one exception, I cannot express my gratitude to these legends in person. Also, I would dearly have liked to go back and ask further questions or obtain more information about the topics we discussed. As a balance, they might well have liked the opportunity to embellish or enhance their answers!

Writing this book has emphasised what characters each and every one was and what an impact they made on the game in their own day and how they shaped the modern game. They were marvellous men of cricket who profoundly influenced the game. I remember Ted Dexter talking to me once about the golden thread that joined one generation to the next, and how that thread was vital to cricket's development. There were sometimes cataclysmic events that threatened that development, and I remember him citing Packer as one of them. Perhaps this book goes some small way to restoring the thread, in that we can learn exactly about the basis of Bodyline, what really happened over the D'Oliveira affair, and how these great players had to overcome obstacles to reach the top.

It is never possible to compare one generation with another, but if cricket is about character there is not the slightest doubt in my mind that each one of them could have been just as great in the modern age as they were in their own. They all possessed an unwavering desire to succeed, and if that desire was sometimes —I might even say usually—shrouded in a cloak of modesty and self-deprecation, their determination still shone through.

As an example, let me conclude by citing a story about Trevor Bailey, told to me by Doug Insole. At Headingley in 1953, England were striving to use up time to prevent a new over by the rampant Australian attack before lunch. Ray Lindwall was preparing to bowl to Jim Laker as the clock ticked towards the 1.30 luncheon interval, while Bailey himself was at the non-striker's end. It was a glorious, hot, sunny summer's day, but that did not prevent him from approaching the umpire just before the first ball of the over was bowled and stating boldly that he wanted to appeal against the light, as technically he was entitled to do.

Frank Chester was astounded, and said that there was nothing wrong with the light. Bailey was aware of that but also knew that the umpires had to consult before delivering a decision about the fitness of conditions for play to continue. Chester walked over to his square-leg colleague, Frank Lee, who was interested to know what the conversation with Bailey was about. When he was told, he sent Chester back with the message that Bailey should get on with the game, or words to that effect. Chester went back to his position and delivered the message to Bailey, who calmly accepted the inevitable but pointed out that by now it was after 1.30. The players left the field for lunch.

But Bailey had not finished. When England needed to prevent Australia scoring 66 to win in 45 minutes (well inside their current scoring rate) with seven wickets in hand, Len Hutton threw the ball to Bailey who came off a very long run and bowled persistently wide of the leg stump. Only 12 overs were bowled in those 45 minutes, Bailey had figures of 1 for 9 in six overs and Australia finished 30 runs short of their target.

Wind the clock forward 60 years to Trent Bridge in 2013, and England were again involved in a tense struggle with Australia. This time, however, it was Australia who were galloping towards the target on the last morning and England had to find some way of halting the momentum. Nine wickets down with 291 on the board chasing another 20, Brad Haddin was winning the match for Australia, having shared a last wicket partnership of 60 with James Pattinson. Stuart Broad had bowled five balls of an over, and with two minutes to go to the interval he appeared to develop the most appalling problems with his boots. Despite none too subtle attempts to waste two minutes, he bowled the last ball and the umpires ordered another over to be bowled. It was a maiden and on the resumption, England took the last wicket to record a 14-run victory.

There are very few actual innovations in the game; only the circumstances in which they appear vary. I like to think that Trevor Bailey, looking down from a celestial commentary box, might have uttered, "I like it!" in suitably enthusiastic tones.

Ralph Dellor's cricketing and writing credentials are impeccable. A very experienced and award-winning broadcaster and author, he has been a player and a cricket coach at university and international levels. Ralph has served on the Sports Council and acted as an advisor to a previous minister for sport. He has written nine successful books about cricket and co-authored a further seven with Stephen Lamb.

Stephen Lamb is also a highly experienced journalist and broadcaster, having worked for the BBC and provided material for Sky and CNN amongst others. Apart from cricket he has covered a wide variety of the major sports for press, radio and television—and still reads the news. As well as sportsmen such as Ian Botham and David Gower, he has also interviewed a number of major political figures.

In 2003, Ralph and Stephen combined their collective sports, broadcasting and journalistic experience to set up Sportsline Media Limited.

NOT OUT
FIRST BALL

The art of being beaten in beautiful places

Roger Morgan-Grenville & Richard Perkins

Foreword by David Gower

'This is a joyful book..a relentlessly entertaining read and
not just for cricket lovers either. Everyone should read it'

NOT OUT FIRST BALL
The art of being beaten in beautiful places

Roger Morgan-Grenville & Richard Perkins

"To field idly at long off in the evening sunshine is to peep back over the wall to when things moved slower, cost less and didn't always need to signify something. At a time of digital abundance, the whole glorious point of cricket is that so much of it is utterly pointless."

Not Out First Ball is a laugh-out-loud manifesto for anyone who has ever silently sobbed at the sight of their off stump cartwheeling off into the distance, or thrown their bat in disgust onto an autumn bonfire.

Roger Morgan-Grenville and Richard Perkins have written a book that is not only funny but also immensely insightful and profound. All cricketers (and maybe even their wives) will identify with the author's experiences and those of his teammates.

"This is a joyful book. In a complicated world of problems and commitments, it demonstrates the importance of having that 'mental green belt', where we make time for doing something that we love. Everyone should read it!"
David Gower, in his Foreword

Hardback • ISBN: 978-1-903071-66-3 • Price: £9.99

Discover more great books at
www.bene-factum.co.uk